Campfires Across Montana
Cooking with Fire

Peggy

Campfires Across Montana Cooking with Fire

Make Cooking Part of Your Adventure!
Make it Easy!

50 years of campfire wisdom

250 recipes and how to cook them with fire
menus and shopping lists for
packing light ~ rivers and rafts
backroads & campers
what to pack, what to wear

maps and facts for
Montana mountains rivers and roads

camping with kids

stories and music

Peggy Racicot

CODE OF MONTANA

Pack it in, Pack it out!
Drown all Fires
Leave no Footprint
Be a good neighbor
Protect our Public Land and Water

Copies of this book may be purchased at local
Montana bookstores and gift shops.
Also, on Amazon.com *(Amazon Prime ships for free)*

For retail sales: please contact me at mpraci@gmail.com

Written, Photographed and Illustrated by Peggy Racicot
2453 West Shore Drive Helena, Montana 59602

ISBN   978-1544962894

TABLE OF CONTENTS
Follow a recipe to find your source,
add and subtract as you please ~ be your own chef

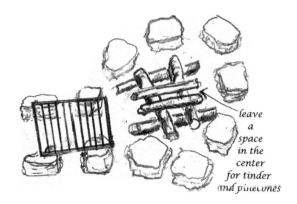

leave
a
space
in the
center
for tinder
and pinecones

the Keyhole

The campfire cook's best friend is a pair of leather gloves

the High -Low

COOKING WITH FIRE
Campfires always bring us together.

If you were raised in Montana you probably already have some understanding of how to cook with fire. I do believe however, even the most knowlegable cooks will find a few tips and a bit of usefull knowledge in this section.

I usually camp with a large group of family or friends. We divide the number of meals by the number of people who will be with us and each person is responsible for only one or two meals for the entire group. Everyone brings their own lunch, and beverages. The bonus *is less work, more play*. Of course we all lend the cook a hand when needed.

The Fire

How to build it, how to maintain it.

Begin by gathering a few rocks and stacking them in 2 rows parallel to each other and just far enough apart for your grill to balance between them. I like to use two smaller grills and position one a little closer to the coals giving me a choice of two cooking temperatures. Choose a couple of flat rocks for the top of your stack to give yourself a little extra space to keep hot pots warm. Try not to use River Rock. BE AWARE that River Rock can explode when over heated and possibly injure someone.

Cook wood is not the same wood you would gather for a blazing evening fire. For cooking you will need to gather medium and small sticks. Try not to collect any green, wet or rotten wood as it will smoke and make your cooking difficult. If you are planning to barbeque, try to use deciduous woods such as aspen and cottonwood if available. These woods provide hot clean coals, while coniferous woods like pine and fir emit some pitch and more smoke.

15

Of course, if you are camping, you know how to start a fire, but sometimes stuff happens. Like your lighter gets lost or it rains. Rain can make the fishing better but not the fire. Not very aesthetic but effective, a quick start to your fire may be obtained by bringing a small squeeze can of lighter fluid. Spray wood before you light. NEVER after the fire is going. NEVER use gasoline, it explodes! I like wood matches and always keep a good supply in a zip lock bag with wax paper and steel wool. Steel wool burns hot and long. I have not tried this but was told you can rub it against your flashlight battery to spark your kindling if you do not have matches. Another trick is to bring a box of birthday candles. Just light two or three candles and tuck them into dry tinder flame side up. You will get a longer flame with less effort.

Build a small fire for cooking and add wood as you need it. Save the big stuff for after dinner. To cook with wood, you need to be able to get close enough to the fire to tend your food. You need coals. The best plan is to build your fire the width of a small grill and twice as long. Then when your coals are ready, you can put your grill on one side and feed small chunks of wood onto the other side maintaining a supply of coals throughout your cooking process. Disturb as little as possible. Constant raking & poking breaks up pockets of heat and lowers your cooking temperature.

When cooking meat on the grill, fats and juices may drip on the coals and cause flames to flare up and burn dinner. To avoid this, trim fat from meat where possible and keep a cup of water handy to sprinkle on the flame. Don't dump water on coals. It will ruin your heat source and push up ashes onto your food. More fun and effective is a water pistol.

For spit cooked meat the coals should be on either side of the meat, but not below, to allow fat to drip.

Smokey Fires

Smokey Fires are often caused by not enough ventilation. Common campground metal fire rings sink into the ground and have no air moving under the fire. Fix it by getting a stick and dig an air vent under the fire ring on at least two sides. Keep in mind that smoke from the flames will make your pots and pans black. If you are patient enough to wait for the coals your cleanup will be easier. You can also wrap the bottom half of the pot with heavy aluminum foil.

When murder is okay!

Kill that fire!   Drown it until you know it's dead!

Move the rocks. There may be living embers underneath. Carefully feel coals with your bare hands to be sure.
Do Not just bury your coals. They can smolder and break out into a wildfire days later ~ a fire that you may be held accountable for.

High Altitude Cooking

High Altitude cooking takes longer. *"As altitude increases and atmospheric pressure decreases, the boiling point of water decreases. To compensate for the lower boiling point of water, the cooking time must be increased. Turning up the heat will not help cook food faster. No matter how high the cooking temperature, water cannot exceed its own boiling point".*
USDA.Gov: search High Altitude Cooking

The boiling temperature of water at sea level is 212 degrees; at a mile high 5,280 feet above sea level, water boils at 201 degrees; at 7,500 feet water boils at about 198 degrees. Because the water is cooler it takes longer to cook the food and therefore you may need to add more water if it boils away before your food is done; so always keep a water bottle handy when cooking to replace the water that has boiled, baked or steamed away. Even if the heat is turned up, the water will simply boil away faster and whatever you are cooking will dry out faster.

Flames to Coals	Cooking Temperature
Small Flame	Water, Coffee, Clear Soups Use a pan or pot because aluminum foil will burn.
Hot Coals	Boiled Foods Bacon, Sausage Fried Potatoes
Medium Hot Coals	Most Meats Steaks, Burgers, Fish, Hot Dogs
Medium to Small Glowing Coals	Eggs, Chili, Thick Soups and Sauces Meals in Aluminum Foil Marshmallows

For example: If you can hold your hand 6 inches above the grill for 4 to 5 seconds your coals are medium hot.

Grilling Time and Temperature

There is no exact timing for campfire cooking. Position your grill 8 to 10 inches above hot coals. Coals are best when there is no flame and you cannot hold your hand 6 inches above the grill. Avoid poking holes in your meat. You want to retain the juice inside. Your meat should be done if it feels firm when you tap on it. Use a sharp knife to cut into the thick part of a steak or chop to see the color, but only once. You don't want the juices to run out. To check poultry slice along the bone or the thickest part of a boneless chicken breast, the juices should run clear. There is a fine line between rare and overdone. Try for the medium and consider that your meat is still cooking during the resting time between the grill and your fork. **You can always put your meat back on the grill if you want it more done but there is no fix for charcoal dried meat.**

Approximate time of cooking for each side				
	Heat of Coals	Rare	Medium	Well Done
Steak 1 inch	Hot	5 to 6 minutes	7 to 8 minutes	10 minutes
Steak 1 ½ inches	Hot	6 to 7 minutes	10 minutes	12 to 15 minutes
Steak 2 inches	Medium to Hot	8 to 10 minutes	15 to 18 minutes	20 minutes
Fish, Small	Medium			5 to 10 minutes
Fish, Large	Medium to Hot			10 to 15 minutes
Pork Chops ¾ inch	Medium to Hot		5 minutes	5 to 7 minutes
Spareribs	Medium		10 minutes	10 to 15 minutes
Roast 4" inches thick	Medium		10 to 20 minutes	30 minutes
Boneless Chicken Breast or Thigh	Medium			8 to 12 minutes
Bone in Chicken Breast or Thigh	Medium			25 to 35 minutes

The Food

I have never made anyone sick with my cooking. OH! I Meant, I have never made anyone sick Of my cooking. Not even the time I packed a full roast beef meal for 12 people into Greyling Lake in the Pioneer Mountains south of Butte. I baked the roast beast with fresh sliced carrots and potatoes at home then sliced the beef and packed it together into two aluminum foil lasagna pans with gravy on the bottom. The pans were sealed with heavy foil and taped shut with duct tape. I didn't want any leaking into my backpack. It took three days for this dinner to thaw enough to heat and eat. We spent that day boot skiing the ice above the lake and enjoyed happy hour with nothing to do but heat our meal. I was the dinner hero. *(Recipe page 202)*

Packing Food

Wrap any frozen food well in heavy aluminum foil and put into seal tight plastic freezer bags. Put these on the inside of your pack where it will stay colder. Pack other cold foods around the frozen food and your other foods around that. When you are not using your pack hang it in a tree to keep the varmints out.

Plan your meals to use fresh meat the first night pre-cooked meat the second, ham or fully cooked sausages the third night, and so on. Canned and dried meats are useful if you will be gone an extended time. Be sure to wash out any empty cans before you put them back in your pack to avoid attracting critters.

PLEASE do not try to burn cans. I really hate walking into a used camp and finding half burned aluminum cans. What is worse, some people think if they can burn the aluminum, they can also burn food cans. These are also the people who leave used toilet paper and baby diapers. Don't be that person! **Crush'm and Pack'm** in pre-used plastic seal tight bags.

Cooking Food

Cook food in the order of heat required for that food item. Begin with foods that can boil such as coffee and soup. Then cook food that you would normally fry like your potatoes and onions, cover and set alongside your grill to keep warm while you grill fish or steaks over hot coals. Sauces, casseroles and puddings must be watched and stirred often to keep from scorching.

To control heat of the fire, adjust the distance of the grill to the coals or start with plenty of coals and use a long stick to push more coals under your food or pull some out. Keep a cup of water handy to sprinkle over any flames that flare up due to fat and juices from meat dripping on the coals. Don't dump water from a cup onto the flame, it will kill your heat source.

Please do not clean your dishes in lakes and streams. Fill a bucket or pan with water and wash dishes away from the bank with biodegradable soap.

About Water

You can get along weeks without food, but your body needs two quarts of water a day to maintain efficiency.

We camped at Lake of the Clouds in the Mission Mountains for two days waiting for the rain to stop because the rocks were too slippery to cross the pass.
Of course, we packed light and used the water from the stream for cooking and coffee. When the rain turned to a misty snow, we decided to abandon the crossing and started to walk out. Two hundred feet from camp we found a dead mountain goat lying on the rocks at the top of the waterfall that drops between Ice Flow and Cliff Lakes.

Moral of the Story: If you can't filter your water, make sure you hard boil it for at least 10 minutes.

Water filters can be purchased in any sporting goods store to use for your personal drinking water but it's very time consuming to filter enough water for all your cooking needs.

To quote a newspaper article from the Montana Standard,

"BACKCOUNTRY USERS BE ON GUARD FOR GIARDIA
"Deerlodge Forest officials are warning recreationist to take precautions this summer against drinking contaminated water. Forest Service spokesman Palmer Bowen said some areas of forest land may have watersheds contaminated with parasitic giardia or other bacteria. No matter how clean lake or stream water appears, it may be contaminated.

To clean mountain water of giardia recreationist can use one of three methods. Hard boiling the water for 10 minutes is the most preferred method for disinfection but chlorination or iodination may be equally effective if done properly.

Water can be chlorinated using Halazone tablets or common bleach. If Halazone is used, which is usually 1 percent available chlorine, 10 drops from an eye dropper should be added to each quart of clear water and 20 to each quart of cold or cloudy water.

If common household bleach is used, which is usually 4-6 percent available chlorine, two drops are needed for every quart of clear water and four drops to every quart of cold or cloudy water. After the chlorine is added, it should be mixed thoroughly by stirring or shaking in a container and let stand for 30 minutes. A slight chlorine odor should be deleted in the water. If not, repeat the procedure and let stand an additional 15 minutes before using.

Treating water with iodine takes longer and requires more care. Iodine crystals or solution should be kept away from skin or eyes and especially kept away from children."

About Eggs

There seems to be a difference of opinion on storing eggs. I have never had a problem with eggs but if I am packing light I pre-cook and freeze my egg casseroles and plan to heat and eat them before they are completely thawed. On the river or the road, I always keep them in a cooler.   Online resources can drive you a little crazy with the overwhelming amount of information. Two good sources of information are: the United States Department of Agriculture: www.fsis.usda.gov and The University of Minnesota extension.umn.edu
extension.umn.edu/food-health-and-nutrition

Why should eggs be refrigerated? Temperature fluctuation is critical to safety. With the concern about Salmonella, eggs gathered from laying hens should be refrigerated as soon as possible. After eggs are refrigerated, they need to stay that way. A cold egg left out at room temperature can sweat, facilitating the movement of bacteria into the egg and increasing the growth of bacteria. Refrigerated eggs should not be left out more than 2 hours.

Should you wash eggs? No. It's not necessary or recommended for consumers to wash eggs and may increase the risk of contamination because the wash water can be "sucked" into the egg through the pores in the shell. When the chicken lays the egg, a protective coating is put on the outside by the hen.

Why do hard-cooked eggs spoil faster than fresh eggs?
When shell eggs are hard cooked the protective coating is washed away, leaving bare the pores in the shell for bacteria to enter and contaminate it. Hard-cooked eggs should be refrigerated within 2 hours of cooking and used within a week.

Dried Egg Mix is a combination of dried whole eggs, nonfat dry milk and soybean oil. Dried egg mix can be purchased in 6-ounce packages which is equal to about 6 eggs. According to package directions: 2½ tablespoons dry whole egg powder mixed with 2½ tablespoons warm water is equal to one egg. *I have to say I have never used this product so I really do not know how it cooks up.*

About Meat

If you like to cook and eat meat, the freezer can be your best friend. I pack the entire portion of one meal in heavy duty aluminum foil then put it into a seal tight plastic freezer bag and freeze it. Because I always do this right after shopping be sure to write the contents of the package on the outside of your freezer bag with a permanent marker. Meat is safe while it is thawing in the cooler but cook ground meats, poultry and fish within one or two days after thawing. Steak or Roasts should be cooked within three to five days if they are in the cooler.

For Backpackers who enjoy meat, play it safe and pre-cook meat then wrap in heavy duty aluminum foil and freeze in seal tight plastic bags. Pack into the interior of your pack where it is more insulated from body heat or the sun on your back. Always bring a length of light rope or parachute cord to hang your pack from a strong branch when you are not using it. Nothing worse than coming back from your day hike and finding your pack destroyed and your food eaten by animals. Remember that even frozen meat is only good for a few days. Salted cured meats like salami and pastrami last longer.

Don't cook ham and bacon together. The water in the ham will keep the bacon from getting crisp. Cook the Bacon first, set aside in aluminum foil, then cook the ham.

Cheese Butter and Oil

Cheese tastes great on everything, and guess what? Cheese was developed by early peoples as a means to preserve and store excess milk. The purpose of cheese is to provide long term food storage without refrigeration.

I like BUTTER, but If a recipe calls for margarine, it is because butter burns more easily. Do not substitute low fat margarine because this is full of water, it will sizzle and not cook well or taste good. For packing light its hard to beat a can of spray canola oil. It doesn't burn as easily as olive oil but still coats your foil and cooking pan in a good way. You just don't really want to put it on your toast.

Yes, Montana made Canola Oil is a good choice for campfire cooking. Sources of information vary because the smokepoint depends on the purity and age of the oil at the time of measurement. Oils with a higher smoke point will be preferred for campfire cooking.

Avocado Oil, refined	520
Safflower Oil	475
Frying Fat	465
Soybean Oil	450
Corn Oil	450
Sunflower Oil	440
Peanut Oil	440
Canola Oil	425
Grapeseed Oil	420
Lard	350
Sesame Oil unrefined 350	350
Olive oil unrefined	331
Vegetable Shortening	325
Walnut oil	320
Butter	300

Dehydrated Food

can really take the weight off your pack but remember, you need water to prepare dehydrated food. Dehydrated and Freeze Dried foods should be soaked before cooking. If you are intent on taking dried beans and lentils soak them overnight and all day at base camp. If you are on the move, pour the beans in a seal tight plastic bag with water and pack them in a bottom side pocket of your pack.

Canned Food

can be useful BUT: because of the garbage and smell usually associated with canned fish and meats, keep it to a minimum. However, if you are going to be on the trail for an extended period of time save them for last. Be sure to wash out the cans with biodegradable soap before crushing them and putting them in a seal tight plastic bag to pack out.

Aluminum Foil

is a must have for campfire cooking. I also like to use a variety of disposable foil pans for cooking. Whenever possible however, I reuse the foil and the pans. When they appear to be garbage PLEASE don't burn them. They smash up easy and small. PACK THEM IN a gallon size seal tight plastic bag and PACK THEM OUT!

Frozen Prepared Food

It's not gourmet but if you have a severe cooking disability, and you like to eat, some of this stuff isn't bad. Don't buy any packages that say Microwaveable, it will be packaged in a plastic container. Only foil packaged food can be heated over a fire. If you are backpacking double wrap all frozen foods in aluminum foil and pack as much together as possible because the more volume of frozen food, the longer it will stay frozen. Some frozen dinners come complete from meat to vegetables and can be heated easily over a campfire in the foil pan they are packaged in. For foods like frozen lasagne buy an extra foil pan of the same size and place pebbles in the bottom of the pan with a little water before you put your food on the grill. The bottom of your food will steam instead of burn.

Food in Bear Country

If you are packing the High Country in June and July, you can often find a bank of snow to cool your food and beverages. Just use a light sleeping bag stuff sack and fill with snow and your food. Be sure to tie it high on a sturdy tree limb to keep the critters out. If you are in bear country, make sure you locate your food stash, grill area and cleaning area a minimum of 200 feet from your sleeping space!!!

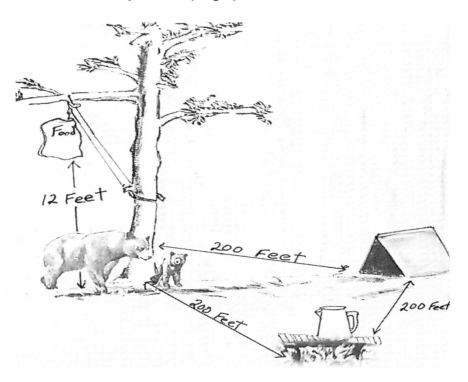

An article Yellowstone Science, a publication by Yellowstone National Park, said there was an average of 1.1 injuries per year in Yellowstone National Park from 1980 to 2014, making the chances of being attacked by a grizzly bear about 1 in 2.7 million visits. It is also important to note that National Park Visitors are heavily fined for not taking the appropriate precautions to deter bears and other wildlife.
Be safe and follow the rules.

Scary Story
because it's true!

We got a late start on a Friday afternoon in September with only the weekend to spend in Yellowstone Park. It was nearly dark when we pulled into a Campground near Quake Lake tired and hungry. The sign at the entrance of the campground warned of recent bear activity in the area but the campground was full except for two tent sites. Both were tent sites near the river. We chose the one with a Big Mama Fir tree with low hanging branches to tuck our 4 man tent under.

We were 28 years old with two young kids. This camp had a round metal fire pit with a flip over grill. While Larry rustled up some wood and got the fire going, the kids and I got the tent up. It was full dark before we had dinner. Pork Chops and baked potatoes on the grill. We were hungry and dinner was good, the smore's were good too.

Because of the bear warning sign we, talked about the "what if's"? Our tent had both a front and a back door so we set the tent far under the branches of the Mama Fir with the back right up against the tree trunk. We packed every bit of food into the jeep and parked it 20 feet from the tent. We burned that grill until it was red hot. If a bear came around, we had a plan.

What we were not thinking of was how strong the lure of cooked pork chops on the grill might be to a grizzly bear.

The kids were sleeping but Larry and I heard the bear coming from the river. We could smell him. We could see him from behind the screen of our tent door. We stayed put in our sleeping bags hoping he would not see our tent. He didn't. He went right to the grill and burned his tongue trying to lick off the smell of the chops.

Angry and injured he roared and shook his head as he tore up a dead stump that we had been sitting on earlier. The debris flew into the air and showered down upon our tent. When he stood at the back of our jeep Cherokee his head was well above the roof as he pushed on the back window trying to get in. The Jeep rocked back and forth but the window held and he wandered off to the next camp.

Those people were in a hard side camper but had hung their pots and pans outside and the Grizzly created a horrible clanging that woke everyone in the campground before he wandered off to terrorize the next camp.

If he came back toward us, I was to take the kids out the back of the tent and up the tree into the thick cover of its heavy branches. Larry went to start the jeep. The Bear heard him and came back to investigate. Larry dropped the keys and fumbled for them on the dark earth. The door was locked. The bear was closer.

The guy in the camper with the pots and pans got his truck lights on and that distracted the bear for a minute before he started back towards Larry. I had the back of the tent open and one child out when Larry finally got the jeep started. It was the only time in my life I thought Glass Packs were cool, and when Larry put the pedal to the metal, that Jeep roared.

The Grizzly ran back across the river. The entire campground honked their horns and clapped. People went back to bed, but I don't think anyone slept well.

The following spring, we read in the newspaper that a young man camping in the same place we had been in September was killed by a Grizzly Bear.

We believed it was the same bear because according to the article in the paper, he had been tracked and studied for several years. He had lost a quarter of his body weight over the winter and was looking for an easy meal.

Beware the Glock, Beware the Rock

Some years back we were camping with our son and friends, one of whom had recently acquired a job in the U.S. Marshalls office. As part of his position he had also acquired a new Glock handgun that the men were doing some target shooting with early in the day. As the campfire waned after midnight I thought it best to head for bed and leave the young men to their conversation which had turned to the population of bears in the area.

Snuggled into my sleeping bag and not yet sleepy I rose just as my husband decided to come in. For some reason we decided to sneak up on the campfire and scare those still at the fire by rustling the bushes and growling like a bear.

We walked along the river which effectively masked our sound but then, needed to make quite a bit of noise to get their attention. When they decided there was definitely ~ something in those bushes and maybe they should get the Glock ... it became time to announce ourselves. ~ Moral of the story, it might not be a good idea to sneak up on campers in the dark.

~ ~ ~ ~ ~

On another occasion I was hiking into Cliff Lake in the Mission Mountains with my brothers, sister and husband. If you have been there you would agree that it is a steep seven to eight hour hike from the car park. All of my brothers are big and strong hikers, but the oldest is especially big and strong. Four hours into the hike we stopped for lunch and one of the brothers thought it would be funny to slow him down a bit by adding some rocks to his already 50 pound pack.

Three more hours into the climb carrying 15 more pounds he took off his pack to arrange the contents as something was poking him in the back. We laughed harder than he did as he started tossing out the rocks. ~ Moral of the story ... trust your instincts. If something doesn't feel right it probably isn't.

Packing Light

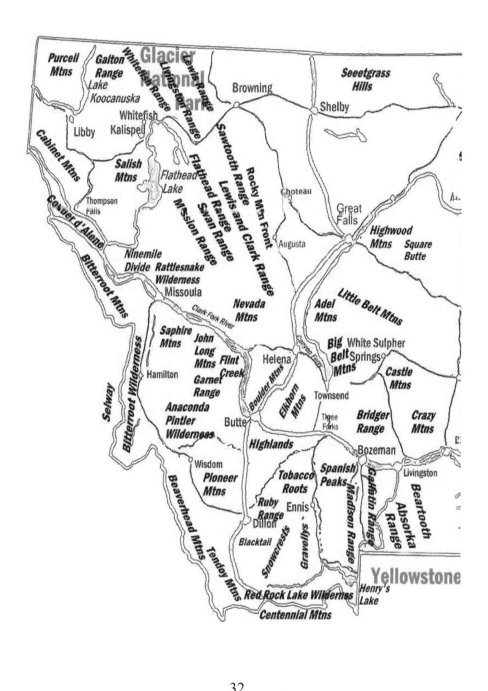

The Mountains Map

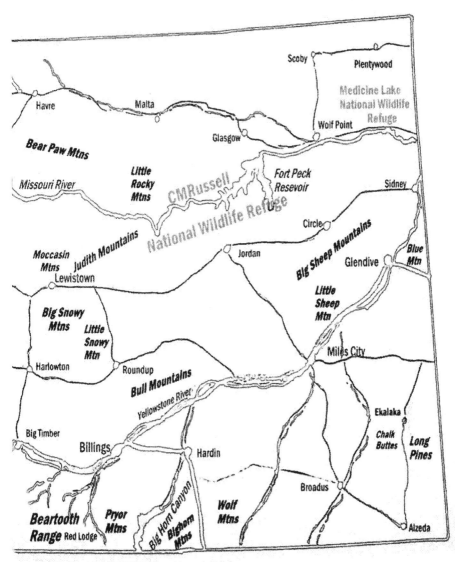

Montana Mountain Ranges Highest Peaks

Wikipedia	Mt.gov/mountain ranges	
Absaroka Range;	Emigrant Peak	10921
Adel Mountains	Adel Mountain	7093
Anaconda Range	West Goat Peak	10793
Bears Paw Mountains	Baldy Mountain	6916
Beartooth Mountains;	Granite Peak	12799
Beaverhead Mountains	Eighteen mile Peak	11125
Big Belt Mountains	Mount Edith	9507
Big Sheep Mountains	Big Sheep Mountain	3590
Big Snowy Mountains	Greathouse Peak	8681
Big Horn Mountains;	Un-named peak	9257
Bitterroot Range	Trapper Peak	10157
Boulder Mountains	Haystack Mountain	8819
Bridger Range	Sacagawea Peak	9650
Bull Mountains	Dunn Mountain	4744
Cabinet Mountains	Snowshoe Peak	8738
Castle Mountains	Elk Peak	8566
Centennial Mountains;	Mount Jefferson	10203
Chalk Buttes	Un-named Peak	4210
Coeur d'Alene Mountains	Cherry Peak	7352
Crazy Mountains	Crazy Peak	11209
Elkhorn Mountains	Crow Peak	9415
Flathead Range	Great Northern	8705
Flint Creek Range	Mount Powell	10168
Gallatin Range	Electric Peak	10969
Galton Range	Poorman Mountain	7832
Garnet Range	Old Baldy Mountain	7511
Gravelly Range	Black Butte	10542
Henrys Lake Mountains	Un-named Peak	10606
Highland Mountains;	Table Mountain	10223
Highwood Mountains	Highwood Baldy	7670

John Long Mountains	Butte Cabin Ridge	8468
Judith Mountains	Judith Peak	6428
Lewis Range	Mount Cleveland	10466
Lewis and Clark Range	Red Mountain	9411
Little Belt Mountains	Big Baldy Mountain	9175
Little Rocky Mountains	Antoine Butte	5743
Little Snowy Mountains	Un-named peak	6260
Livingston Range	Kintla Peak	10101
Long Pines	Tri-Point Lookout	4120
Madison Range	Hilgard Peak	11297
Mission Range	McDonald Peak	9820
Nevada Mountains	Black Mountain	8330
Ninemile Divide	Stark Mountain	7352
North Moccasin	Un-named peak	5602
Pioneer Mountains	Tweedy Mountain	11154
Pryor Mountains	Big Pryor Mountain	8786
Purcell Mountains	Northwest Peak	7705
Rattlesnake Mountains	McLeod Peak	8620
Reservation Divide	Ch-paaa-qn Peak	7996
Ruby Range	Un-named Peak	9391
Salish Mountains	McGuire Mountain	6991
Sapphire Mountains	Kent Peak	9010
Sawtooth Range	Rocky Mountain	9392
Snowcrest Range	Sunset Peak	10581
South Moccasin Mountains	Un-named peak	5798
Spanish Peaks	Gallatin Peak	11015
Swan Range	Holland Peak	9356
Sweet Grass Hills	West Butte	6983
Tendoy Mountains	Ellis Peak	9699
Tobacco Root Mountains	Hollowtop Mountain	10604
Whitefish Range	Nasukoin Mountain	8086
Wolf Mountains	Un-named peak	5450

PACKING LIGHT

Be the Hero

Freeze a can of beer per person, pack them to base camp and toss your buddies a cold one. *"Plan B," toss* them to your buddies in the parking lot and let them pack their own beer to base camp.

Don't pack more than you need but remember, at the end of the day you will be hungry and tired. Make supper part or your adventure. Something your group will talk about when they mention that trip into the Missions or Beartooth. Lighten your pack by transferring contents of glass or canned foods into plastic containers. Use dry milk powder for cooking and powdered juices for beverages. Pre-cook meat and wrap in several layers of aluminum foil to insulate. Freeze in plastic seal lock bags then use the foil to cook with. Purchase an insulated freezer bag to transport your meat.

Thinking about dried beans and lentils? I was 18 and it was my first trip into the Mission Mountains. It was near midnight when we got to our first camp at Island Lake halfway up the mountain. We had packed Sub Sandwiches because we knew it would be a late camp. The second night after a long day of hiking to Ice Flo Lake and McDonald Peak the menu was ham soup with dried beans and lentils. Not so good. Dried beans and lentils need to soak all day or overnight to be edible. So, if dried beans are on your menu, put them in a cook pot filled with water after breakfast and let them soak All Day ~ I mean ALLL Day Long! When you return to base camp tired and hungry you can start them to simmer over medium coals for an hour or more before they are ready to eat. High altitudes make this a slowwww process and requires lots of water.

Packing List   Group Equipment

Coffee Pot, wrapped in plastic grocery bag to keep your pack clean from the inevitable campfire black.
Fry Pan with High Sides, wrapped in plastic grocery bag.
Spatula, Cooking Fork, Sharp Knife, can opener
Heavy Aluminum Foil (cut into useable sizes and folded)
Campfire Grill 16x8, Wooden Matches, & Wax Paper (cut and folded)
Tent (two to four man)
Parachute Cord or small rope
Water Purifier, Filter
Folding Plastic Water Bucket
Biodegradable Soap & scrubber sponge
FIRST AID KIT: chewable baby aspirin, Tylenol, polysporin, sterile pads, flexible band aids, butterfly bandaids, ace bandage, surgical tape, sewing kit, tooth floss, eye wash, tweezers, antiseptic wash (We love Band-Aid brand, in the blue bottle. *It's a topical pain killer, works for bug bites too.*

Your Pack

Water Bottle and an eye dropper bottle of chlorine bleach **WELL MARKED AND LABELED**
Wood Matches, Birthday Candles, Wax Paper folded into squares and packed in quart size seal tight plastic bag.
Leather Gloves for cooking & camp chores
Gallon size plastic freezer bags for garbage
Tin Plate or Frisbee with paper plates
Coffee cup is also soup bowl & wine glass
Sharp knife, fork and spoon, Combination can opener & corkscrew
2 Large flour sack dish towels, one for dishes and one for your personal needs.
2 Large Garbage Bag to cover your pack if it rains and to use as a ground cover to prepare your food on.
Coarse Ground Coffee, cocoa, powdered Gatorade, Energy Bars, Peanut Butter

Personals

What to Wear

Layer: Tank top, T Shirt and Polar Fleece sweater
Lightweight canvas pants or your favorite stretchies
Hiking boots & good hiking socks
Sunglasses and hat

What to Pack

1 pair of socks per day if you don't like blisters
Light weight sweatpants   double as jammies if you are sharing a tent
Shorts, Water Sandals,
Rain Gear, Fleece Jacket, also works as a pillow.   A pillowcase for your fleece is nice
Leather gloves, for camp chores and glacier skiing
Toothpaste, Toothbrush, Comb, Wash Cloth Baking soda toothpaste *baking soda relieves pain if you are stung by a bee in the mouth, yes it happened to me.*
Flexible bandaids, chewable baby aspirin (in case you swallow a bee) ibuprofen, eye drops, tooth floss, sewing needle, lemon grass essential oil to repel insects
Mirror (car visor mirrors are a good size)
Biodegradable shampoo, doubles as body wash
Sunscreen and lip sunscreen, bug repellent
Travel size Kleenex for Toilet Paper
Sleeping bag and self-inflating sleeping pad
2 small flashlights with fresh batteries
Good Book, Deck of Cards, Harmonica, Frisbee
Camera and film. Extra camera battery
First Aid minimum: Polysporin, Skin Tape, Aspirin
Light weight folding Camp Chair, tie it to the back of your pack.
Fishing Rod and fly's and lures. Fishing License

Shop and Go Food

Frozen Foods are a convenience that cannot be ignored. They usually have enough preservatives to keep from spoiling for several days. Double wrap all frozen foods in aluminum foil and pack in an insulated freezer bag. Pack as much together as possible because the more volume of frozen food the longer it will stay frozen. **Frozen Dinners** cannot compete with homemade for taste and nutrition but may be convenient for very time stressed people. Some are complete from meat to vegetables and heat easily over a campfire in the aluminum tray they are packaged in. Do not purchase foods that say they are microwaveable. These foods are generally packaged in plastic containers that cannot be heated over a fire without transferring the food into your metal pots and pans. Bring one extra disposable aluminum pan (lasagna size) to act as your oven. Place pebbles in the bottom of this extra pan and fill with water to the top of your pebbles. Place this pan on your grill over medium coals. The bottom of your dinner will steam instead of burn.

If you are cooking for a crowd buy family size packages of Turkey or Roast Beef in Gravy and serve with instant mashed potatoes.

Have your pork chop and eat it too. Be mindful that some of the best Frozen Food might be made in your town. If you are anywhere near Butte or Anaconda pick up a bag of frozen pork chop sandwich patties or tamales. I like frozen breakfast pasties too.

If you know you will be hiking through waterless stretches of trail **Oranges and Seedless Grapes** are incredibly thirst quenching and, I think, worth the weight.

Instant oatmeal if you must but **Whole Rolled Oats** or Stone Ground Oatmeal is so much better. Cook with raisins and walnuts. Yummy.

Other foods to consider on your grocery list might be complete pancake mix, powdered milk, canned mandarin oranges, dried prunes, coffee and tea, cocoa, powdered energy drinks like Gatorade®.

Pita Bread, English Muffins, Tortillas and Baguettes pack well
Peanut butter, Salami, Mustard, Cheese
Apples, Oranges, crunchy Baby Dill Pickles
Energy Bars, Cheese Sticks, or Mini Cheeses.
Candy bars, Snickers® Bars travel well and can be frozen,
Cookies and Crackers with Cheese or Peanut butter.
Fruit and nut mix, beef jerky.
Instant Potatoes, Rice and Pasta mixes that come with seasoning packets. Instant soup mixes.
Dried Oriental meals are a great change from the usual
Fully cooked smoked Kielbasa or Brats
Tuna Fish packed in Water
Processed Canned Meats like chicken, beef or pork.

Heavy aluminum foil, Seal tight plastic freezer bags. Wood matches, Wax paper (for fire starting), Biodegradable dish soap, Crisco® hard vegetable shortening for cooking, or margarine which does not burn as fast as real butter.
Margarine in a squeeze bottle like ketchup that's easy to pack.
Seal tight plastic freezer bags, both gallon size and quart size.

Don't forget a few personals, like travel Kleenex, sunscreen, tooth floss, butterfly bandaids, wood matches.

Frisbees aren't just to play with.

They also Slap flies and Hold your paper plate.

Lazy Boy Shop and Go Mountain Menu

Four people on the mountain, three days
TOOLS:
  8 cup coffee pot
  camp grill
  serving spoon
  cook gloves
  insulated frozen food bag
  High sided fry pan or disposable alluminum cake pan.

Pack all frozen foods together on the bottom of one pack.
Pack deli meat, butter and cheeses on top of those.

OTHER STUFF:
  Heavy aluminum foil,
  Spray can of butter flavor canola oil
  Paper plates
  Seal tight plastic freezer bags both gallon and quart size
      Don't buy the zipper bags, they do not seal tight.
  Wood matches
  Wax paper (for fire starting)
  Biodegradable dish soap

Don't forget a few personals: coffee cup, knife and fork,
frisbee to hold your paper plate, travel Kleenex, sunscreen,
tooth floss, butterfly bandaids, wood matches.

Breakfast

Coffee, Coarse ground (if you are not using a filter)
cream, sugar, cocoa, Instant Protein Powder like Whey

8 pack Sausage Egg & Cheese Biscuits Fully Cooked

1 package of 12 Jimmy Dean Pancakes and Sausage
  on a stick, optional: small bottle of maple syrup

Quaker Steel Cut Oats or Quick 3-minute Oatmeal with
Cranberries and Blueberries, 8 Packets Per Box

Lunch & Snacks

Grapes and tangerines
Cheese slices; swiss, cheddar, pepper jack
Lunch meat
   cured meats like salami and summer sausage last longer
Tortillas for wraps
   good for breakfast lunch and dinner, buy a 12 pack
Peanut butter, Squeeze jelly
Pickles, Mustard
Party rye bread, can deviled ham spread, cheese slices,
   can opener, *crush and pack your can in a plastic bag*
Energy bars
Snickers candy bars® travel well and include peanut protein
powdered Gatorade® to mix with your water.

Tin Foil Dinners

Wrap individual meals in non-stick heavy aluminum foil and cook on the grill over hot coals. Hamburger will be done in about 30 minutes, Pork and chicken about 45 minutes. Flip dinner package when about half done. Serve in foil.

Hamburger Steak and Potatoes
Frozen hamburger patties
Frozen hash browns
Package Brown Gravy

Remember the cooks' leather gloves.

Don't forget the spray cooking oil.

Pork Chops and Beans
Thin sliced pork chops
Pork 'n Beans
Yellow mustard

Ham Steak, Mashed Potatoes, Green Beans
Ham Steak, Fully Cooked and frozen if possible
Frozen Baked Scalloped Potatoes
Note: dried package potatoes weigh less but require water and a pan to cook and more time ~ weight vs effort?

Meatball Sub
Frozen Meatballs in marinara sauce, family size
Hoagie Sandwich buns
Sliced Mozzarella cheese

Tuna Melt
4 people ~ tools: non-stick heavy aluminum foil, can opener, large seal tight plastic bag, fork

2 - 7 ounce cans Solid White Albacore Tuna in Water
6 packets Mayonnaise (fast food size)
8 ounces shredded Medium Cheddar Cheese
2 crunchy Whole Dill Pickles
4 Pocket Pita's

Open tuna and drain ALL water. Chop dill pickles into small pieces. Combine tuna, mayonnaise, pickles and cheese in a plastic bag and stir together. Fill interior of Pita Bread with Mix. Wrap in Foil and heat on grill over medium hot coals turning occasionally.

How to Open a Can with a Metal Spoon

Hold the can firmly on a flat steady place. Like a flat rock or stump. Use the other hand to postion the tip of the spoon against the inner lid of the can at a 90 degree angle. Rub the tip of the spoon in the groove where the lid meets the can.

Rub the tip of the spoon back and forth over a small area until the friction thins the metal and the spoon rubs through the lid. Move on to another small area until you have rubbed through the entire lid. Dig the spoon under the lid and pry upwards. The lid will be very sharp so use gloves to protect your hand. Dispose of lid and can in seal tight plastic garbage bag and pack it out.

PACKING LIGHT MENU's

4 Nights on the Mountain

page	Breakfast
43	Café Mocha Mix
50	Corned Beef Hash and Eggs
44	Fruit and Nuts Overnight Cereal
51	Summit Cakes
45	Apple Peanut Quesadilla's

	Lunch, Snacks Appetizers
	Wraps: Flour Tortillas, Pastrami, Provolone Cheese, Pickles, Mustard
	Salami, Sliced Cheese
	Peanut Butter & Apples,
	Energy Bars, Fruit & Nut Mix

	Dinner
58	Camp Mac & Cheese with Ham Steak and Green Beans
70	Backpackers Red Spaghetti garlic bread
65	Roasting Hot Sub
71	Beer Brats & Kraut

	Dessert
75	Huckleberry Danish
73	Limoncello & Berries Cake
	5 oz. bag dried cherries, extra dark chocolate
87	Russian Tea & Malano Cookies

One Pan or No Pan Breakfast

"IT WAS NOT ME THAT WOKE THEM.
IT WAS THE COLUMBIAN, I SWEAR!"

Campfire Coffee

Tools: 8 cup coffee pot,
leather gloves to handle the hot pot

6 cups of water plus ½ cup COLD water
½ cup coarse ground coffee
(finely ground coffee will be thick and muddy)
Don't forget the Orphan Girl   : o }

Bring 6 cups of water to a boil in the coffee pot
over hot coals. Hard Boil for 10 minutes if the
water has not been purified, cover with a lid so
the water doesn't evaporate as quickly. Move
the pot to the side of the grill and add coffee.
Allow to set about ten minutes. Pour 1/2 cup
of cold water over the coffee grounds to settle
them to the bottom of the pot.

Café Mocha Mix

⅓ cup instant coffee
1 cup dehydrated whole milk powder
½ cup instant non dairy creamer
½ cup powdered sugar
¼ cup instant hot cocoa mix

At home, mix all ingredients in 2 quart seal tight plastic bag.
To prepare: Boil water in coffee pot over hot coals for 10
minutes if not purified. Fill cup with boiling water and stir in
2 tablespoons of Café Mocha Mix.

Fruit and Nuts Overnight Cereal

4 people ~ tools: Tin Coffee Cups or Cook pot with lid or make individual servings in tin coffee cups.

AT HOME: mix all ingredients except water into a quart size seal tight freezer bag

2 cups rolled oats or steel cut oats
½ cup powdered whole milk
½ cup chopped almonds, walnuts or pecans
½ cup sunflower seeds
½ cup coconut
½ cup raisins, craisins or dried fruit
3 cups water
IN CAMP optional: powdered whole milk, butter, honey

IN CAMP: Pour the oatmeal mix into the cook pot, cover and let set overnight. You can also put a rock on top of the lid to be sure no critters will get into your breakfast. Serve cold. Or reheat in the morning by adding butter and milk to the bottom of the pot before heating. Serve with hot milk, butter, honey.

Toasted Peanut Butter and Jelly

4 people ~ tools: heavy aluminum foil, slicing knife and plate

1 loaf hearty Whole Grain Bread. *I like Dave's Killer Bread.*
16 ounce jar of peanut butter
10 ounce jar jelly. *I like Smuckers® Simply Fruit*
6 ounce can of canola spray oil with butter flavor
4 squares of heavy aluminum foil

Spread the peanut butter all the way to the edge. You are hungry so don't make it a thin spread. Spread the other side with jelly. Spray the outside of your sandwich with butter flavored oil. Wrap in heavy aluminum foil and toast both sides on the grill over hot coals until your peanut butter is warm.

Apple Peanut Quesadilla's
4 people ~ tools: 4 squares aluminum foil

2 large apples
6 tablespoons peanut butter
8 slices medium cheddar cheese
4 large flour tortillas
Spray oil

Spray oil on one side of each tortilla then spread the other side with peanut butter. Place on top of the open foil. Slice apples in small chunks or thin slices and distribute on top of peanut butter. Put 2 slices of cheese on each tortilla. Place on the grill over hot coals until peanut butter starts to bubble and cheese starts to melt. Fold in half and heat until cheese and peanut butter start to ooze out.

Breakfast Kabobs
4 people ~ tools: 4 sharpened green willow sticks

1 pound smoked fully cooked Kielbasa sausage
       sliced into one inch pieces
4 pre-baked potatoes, quartered.
1 onion, quartered and separated.
2 oranges, peeled and separated into sections
optional: catsup

Arrange on sharpened stick in this order. Kiebasa, onion, potato, orange section, Kiebesa. This way the potato and onion are surrounded by something juicy to keep them from burning. Turn slowly over hot coals until heated through.

Breakfast Parfait
4 people ~ coffee cups or clear plastic beverage glasses

2 cups fresh berries
2 cups plain yogurt
2 tablespoons honey
2 cups chunky granola

Stir the honey into the plain yogurt. Layer the yogurt, granola and berries into the glasses in two layers.

Ham Pineapple Donut Kabobs
3 people ~ tools: Slicing knife, 3 sharpened willow sticks, fork, can opener

1 large and thick Ham Steak
1 15 ounce can Pineapple Chunks in 100% juice
1 16 ounce bag Plain Donut Holes

At Home: Repackage pineapple into seal tight ziplock bag. Enjoy the pineapple juice : }   Slice ham into squares the size of the Pineapple Chunks and repackage into seal tight bag.

In Camp:
Thread the Pineapple, Ham, Donut, Ham, Pineapple on the stick in that order so the donut is not wet from the pineapple. Heat over warm coals, marshmallow style.

No Pan Scrambles
4 people ~ tools: heavy aluminum foil, slicing knife and plate

1 pound fully cooked polish sausage or kielbasa
4 baked potatoes or hash browns.
4 eggs
1 large onion
1 large green pepper
1 large tomato
4 large squares of nonstick aluminum foil
Olive oil
salt and pepper

At Home: Pre-bake potatoes in the microwave.

In Camp: Drizzle olive oil onto the 4 large squares of aluminum foil. Slice sausage, potatoes, onion, pepper and tomato onto the foil in equal portions. Crack eggs over each portion and stir a little.   Salt & pepper and drizzle a little more oil around the edges of the eggs. Wrap foil around food sealing the edges well. Heat over medium coals turning often to avoid scorching.

Clam Scramble
4 people ~ tools: 1 fry pan, spatula, can opener

1 8 ounce can minced clams, drained of juice
1 4 ounce package cream cheese
4 tablespoons butter or margarine
1 16 ounce carton of liquid eggs (pack with other cold food)

Melt margarine in fry pan and stir in clams and cream cheese. Add eggs when cream cheese has softened. Scramble, the eggs turning once or twice until done. Over stirring will make your eggs tough and dry.

Bundle of Breakfast
4 people ~ tools: 4 squares heavy aluminum foil

16 ounce package frozen potatoes Obrien
    if the potatoes thaw, they are fine for a couple of days
6 thick ham slices cut into bite size pieces
4 eggs
4 tablespoons margarine
 Salt, pepper, catsup or Franks red hot sauce

Coat each square of foil well with margarine. Divide potatoes and ham equally onto foil. Salt and pepper. Crack egg over each portion and mix a little. Fold into bundles, seal edges and cook over medium hot coals for 10 minutes, turning often to avoid scorching.

Meal in a Muffin
4 people ~ tools: 1 fry pan, spatula

1 - 2 English Muffins per person, sliced in half
1 - 2 Ham slices per-person
1 - 2 cheese slices per person
1 - 2 eggs per person
4 tablespoons margarine
Durkees ® dressing or deli mustard and mayonnaise

Use one half of the margarine to fry the eggs sunny side up. Slide 2 slices of ham under each egg and place cheese on top of the egg to melt. Toast muffins on the grill over coals, not flame. Spread remaining margarine on the toasted muffins. Slide one half of each muffin under the ham, egg & cheese. Top with Durkees ® and the other half of each muffin.

Trout with Bacon and Biscuits
4 people ~ tools: 1 fry pan or griddle, spatula, tin coffee cup

4 freshly caught brook trout
1 pound bacon
lemon wedges
salt, pepper

Clean the trout, Remove heads but leave the tail. Wipe with a damp cloth. Cook bacon over medium coals in a fry pan until not quite crispy. Pour most of the bacon grease into the tin coffee cup. Pile bacon to one side and lay the fish into the hot greased pan. Place one slice of bacon inside the cavity of each fish . Fry three to four minutes on each side. Sprinkle with salt and pepper. Top with lemon. After cooking, pour leftover bacon grease into fire to burn off.

Scratch Biscuits
4 people ~ tools: 1 fry pan with lid

2 cups biscuit mix
1/4 cup powdered milk
1 teaspoon all natural butter buds or popcorn seasoning
Spay vegetable oil

At Home: Combine mix, milk and seasoning in quart size zipper lock bag.

In Camp: Gently stir 1/2 cup water into the bag of biscuit mix. Press the dough into flat circles. Spray fry pan with oil and cook over medium hot coals, turning them when light brown.

Corned Beef Hash and Eggs
2 people ~ tools: 1 fry pan, spatula

4 slices bacon
1 box dehydrated hash brown potatoes
1 red onion, diced
1 pound cooked corned beef
    (deli corned beef also works but ask for thicker slices)
4 eggs
salt, pepper
2 cups water

Open the box of dehydrated potatoes carefully without tearing the inside plastic bag. Fill the bag of potatoes with water and allow to set for ½ hour to 1 hour.
Cut each piece of bacon into 4 pieces and cook bacon in frypan over hot coals.
Drain ALL water from the potatoes and squeeze out any remaining water with a paper towel. Carefully add potatoes to hot bacon grease taking care that bacon grease does not splatter on you.
Cut corned beef into pieces and and mix into potatoes with chopped onion.. Push potatoes to the side of the pan to keep warm. Crack eggs into the pan and cook on low heat until whites are fully cooked but yolks are just a little runny.

A high sided fry pan that is not too heavy may be the only pan you will ever need breakfast through dinner. I like stainless steel because it is easy to clean with sand and soap on a sponge, others prefer a non stick coating. Pack it in a plastic grocery bag when you're not ready to clean the burn off the outside.

Summit Cakes

"Top O The Mountain to Ya"

This mix will feed 4 people for 3 meals
tools: 1 frypan, spatula, large spoon, 2 gallon size seal tight
plastic bags to mix your pancake batter in OR a mixing bowl

AT HOME:
Mix the following ingredients in a zip lock bag for packing

3 cups Complete Wheat Blend pancake mix
1½ cup old fashioned rolled oats (not instant oatmeal)
½ cup powdered whole milk
½ cup brown sugar
2 cups raisins and/or craisins
1 cup walnut pieces, not whole walnuts

IN CAMP:

2 cups summit cake mix
2 cups water
1 Tablespoon canola oil
optional: sliced bananas, huckleberries
¼ cup canola oil
Butter, Peanut Butter, Jelly

To prepare for 4 people, pour 2 cups Summit Cake Mix into a gallon size seal tight plastic bag. Add 2 cups of water and 1 tablespoon of canola oil. Stir until you get rid of the large lumps of mix, it can still be a little lumpy.

Briefly heat fry pan over hot coals with enough oil to coat the bottom of your pan. *Your pan is ready when drops of water sizzle and disapear.* Spoon in 3 circles of pancake mix. When the top of the cake starts to bubble and dry, flip each cake only once. Serve with butter, Peanut Butter and jelly. Repeat until your batter is gone

Lunch, Snacks & Energy Food

Fruit – oranges are the best for packing. They take a lot of abuse and are a great thirst quencher. Grapes are also great if you pack them in your coffee pot.

Grapes and Jarlsberg Cheese slices

Salami Rolls with Cheese Sticks and Baby Dill Pickles,

Peanut Butter and Jelly Tortilla Rolls

Apple Slices and Celery Sticks with Peanut Butter

Bologna, Yellow Mustard, Crackers

Dried Fruit and Nut Mixes, like cranberries and walnuts

Snack Crackers and Humus

Chinese Style Pork with Mustard

Sandwich's and Fixins'

Breads that will not squish easlly or are already flat
like party rye, pita bread, tortillas or french bread.

Add: Deli meats: Pastrami, Salami, Roast Beef, Turkey
Sliced Cheeses, Cream Cheese, Pickles, Deli Mustard

Tortillas with Stuff

Deli Roast Beef, Tomato, Cheddar Cheese, Mustard

Sliced Chicken, Muenster Cheese, Durkees Dressing

Ham, Swiss Cheese, Mustard

Tomato, Avocado, Cream Cheese, Onions, Black Olives

Corned Beef Pickle Wrap
4-5 people

16 ounce jar dill pickles spears
   (repackaged into seal tight plastic bags)
16 ounce thin sliced deli corned beef
 8 ounces sliced swiss cheese mustard optional

Wrap corned beef and swiss slices around pickles.
Squirt with mustard

Bake your own Energy Bars
Bake at home and pack in seal tight plastic bags

4 cups old fashioned rolled oats
1 cup broken peanut pieces
1 cup raisins
1 cup coconut
1 cup peanut butter
¼ cup margarine (not low fat because of the water added)
1 bag miniature marshmallows

Toast old fashioned rolled oats on a cookie sheet in the oven. Place the cookie sheet on the bottom rack and turn on low broil. Leave the oven door slightly ajar to let out steam. Stir often to keep from burning. This will only take a few minutes so watch them closely. Remove from oven when lightly browned.

Melt margarine and peanut butter in a large soup pan on top of the stove over medium heat. Stir in the marshmallows. When the marshmallows are melted. Stir in oats, peanuts, raisins and coconut. Pour into a greased 9x12 inch cake pan and press down with a spoon to compact. Allow to cool then cut into squares.

No Bake Peanut Butter Bars

Make at home and store in zipper lock bags

1 cup extra crunchy peanut butter
½ cup honey
2 cups old fashioned oatmeal
½ cup toasted coconut
1 cup Craisins or raisins

Combine the peanut butter and honey in a medium saucepan and warm over low heat. Stir constantly until mixed thoroughly. Remove from heat and stir in the oatmeal and craisins. Press into a 9×9 inch ungreased pan and let cool. Cut into bars and store in zipper bags. It is not necessary to refrigerate.

Humus

Serve in Pita Bread or spread on a baguette

2 12-ounce cans of chickpeas
2 Tbsp olive oil
6 Tbsp sesame tahini
2 tablespoons lemon juice
Your choice of seasonings:
    My favorite humus seasoning is Valentina or Louisiana Hot Sauce some people prefer garlic or ranch seasoning.

At Home: Combine chickpeas, oil, tahini and lemon juice in a food processor and pulse until well blended. If the Humus is too thick add a tablespoon of water. Spoon into a bowl and add seasonings to taste. Store it in a zip lock bag.

Pita Bread and Beans

4 people ~ tools: Knife

1 16 ounce can of black beans
1 16 ounce can of Rositas fat free refried beans
1 16 ounce can Fire Grilled Southwestern Corn
4 slices of Pita Bread

At home: Drain the liquid from the black beans and the corn. Combine the beans and the corn in one quart size seal tight plastic bag. Repackage the refried beans in another seal tight plastic bag.

On the Trail: Slice the Pita Bread in half and open the center like a boat. Spread the inside of each Pita half with refried beans then fill with black beans and corn.

Peanut Butter and Apple Pita's

4 people ~ tools: Knife

4 slices of Pita Bread
1 jar of peanut butter
4 apples

Slice Pita's in half and open the center. Spread peanut butter inside the bread. Chop or slice apples into the open pita.

Smoked Gouda and Prosciutto Wraps

4 people ~ tools: Knife

8 ounce package of sliced Gouda or other soft cheese
12 ounce of deli prosciutto or thin slice ham
4 whole dill pickles sliced in half lengthwise

Wrap cheese and meat around pickle slices

Turkey Pita
3 to 6 sandwiches ~ tools: slicing knife

3 whole wheat pitas
8 ounce chive and onion cream cheese spread
16 ounces thin sliced deli turkey
1 tomato sliced
1 cucumber peeled and sliced

Slice Pitas in half and spread inside with cream cheese.
Fill with turkey tomato and cucumber.

Ham and Swiss Ciabatta
4 sandwiches

4 Ciabatta Rolls
16 ounce package thin sliced honey ham
8 ounce package baby swiss cheese
6 ounce bottle honey mustard
12 ounce jar crunchy dill pickle slices *(repackaged into seal tight plastic bags)*

Slice rolls in half, spread with mustard and layer ingredients.

Shrimp Cocktail
4 people ~ tools: slicing knife, can opener, forks
4 plastic cocktail glasses

2   4 ouncs cans medium shrimp
1 10 ounce plastic jar spicy cocktail sauce
2 stalks celery, diced
1 Lemon, Lemon pepper

Open shrimp and drain all liquid. Divide into cocktail glasses.
Dice celery and mix with shrimp. Top with cocktail sauce.
Sprinkle with lemon pepper, garnish with lemon slices.

One Pan or No Pan Dinners

Foil Baked Trout
4 people ~ tools: aluminum foil

4 whole brook trout, cleaned and beheaded
Salt and pepper
2 tablespoons butter, cut into 4 pieces
1 lemon, thinly sliced

Place each trout on a sheet of aluminum foil 4 inches longer than the fish. Lightly salt and pepper inside the fish cavity and add butter and lemon slices. Fold up sides of foil around fish and seal leaving a little opening on each side for steam to escape. Place on the grill over hot coals. Grill fish for about 10 minutes per thickness on each side or until fish is flaky. Excessive turning will cause the fish to break apart.

Tobacco Root Mountains

Camp Mac & Cheese with Ham Steak

4 people ~ tools: 8x12 disposable aluminum cake pan
heavy aluminum foil for pan lid

1 or 2 Boneless fully cooked Ham Steak
Enough for 4 people ~ If its not pre-frozen pack it with
your other frozen foods
1 8-ounce package dried pasta shells
3 cups water
4 ounces Velveeta® cheese, cubed
4 ounces Muenster cheese, cubed
¼ cup powdered whole milk
¼ cup margarine
Salt and pepper to taste

Optional: 2 cans of green beans, repackaged in seal tight bag

Grease the sides and bottom of the aluminum cake pan well with margarine and slice whatever is left into the bottom of the pan. Pour in the water then stir in the powdered milk. Place on the grill over medium hot coals. When the margarine is melted and the water starts to simmer, pour in the pasta shells. There should be enough water to completely cover the pasta. Add more water if needed. Allow to cook until pasta is tender. Drain excess water but leave pasta wet. Mix the cheese into the pasta gently without over stirring. If you are adding beans, spread them out on top of the mac n cheese before the ham.

While you are waiting for the pasta to cook, slice the ham steak into 4 quarters and grill lightly. You do not want to dry out your ham! Place the ham on top of pasta and cheese mix. Cover tightly with aluminum foil so no steam escapes. By now you should have medium coals. Your meal should be ready in about 30 minutes. Adjust heat as needed.

Roast Beef and Mashed Potatoes
4 people ~ tools: 2 aluminum foil cake pans, 3 squares of aluminum foil, cooks leather gloves

2 pounds thick sliced deli roast beef, <u>unseasoned</u>
1 ounce package dried beef gravy mix
1 ounce package dried au jus mix
1 family size package 8 oz. Idaho Instant Mashed Potatoes
6 cups filtered water (or hard boiled for 10 minutes)
12 ounce package frozen green beans
Canola oil or margarine for green beans
¼ pound real butter or margarine for potatoes
1 six ounce package French's original Crispy Fried Onions

If you are not using filtered water hard boil 6 cups of water in your clean coffee pot for 10 minutes.

Pour two cups of water into one cake pan and stir in the gravy and au jus mix. Cut roast beef into large bite size pieces. Add roast beef to the gravy mix. Cover with foil and place on the grill over hot coals to simmer. Stir occasionally.

Wrap green beans in foil and drizzle with canola oil. Place on grill to heat, turning occasionally.

When meat and beans are hot place the second foil pan on the grill over hot coals and pour in 4 cups of water. Stir in the instant mashed potatoes and dot with butter. *~ They will be instantly ready so don't do this until you are ready to eat.*

Serve roast beef and gravy over the top of potatoes

Top green beans with crispy fried onions.

Turkey and Stuffing with Vegetables
4 people ~ tools: 4 12-inch pieces heavy aluminum foil

8 thin slices of turkey breast cutlets
1   6 ounce package stove top Turkey Stuffing Mix
1   10 ounce package frozen broccoli, cauliflower
    and carrot blend
1 ½ cups water
4 Tablespoons butter
Dried Rosemary and Sage Seasoning
Olive oil

Open the box of stuffing without tearing the inner plastic
pouch. Pour in water and shake up to moisten the stuffing.
Allow to set while you divide the vegetables among the foil
squares. Drizzle the vegetables with olive oil and sprinkle on
the seasonings. Place 2 slices of turkey on top of the
vegetables then divide the moistened stuffing mix on top of
the turkey.   Wrap and seal the foil around the turkey and
vegetables. Place on grill over medium-low coals, turning
occasionally. Cook about 40 minutes or until stuffing is warm.
Be careful when opening the packages so you are not burned
by the escaping steam.

Wild Turkeys in Montana
*Montana falls outside the wild Turkey's ancestral range
and it is not native to Montana. When the Montana
Department of Fish and Game decided to introduce
Turkeys into Montana, it selected the Merriam Turkeys as
the best choice to achieve success. In 1954, department
biologists introduced 13 Colorado birds into the Judith
Mountains of central Montana. A second release was
made in 1955 when 18 turkeys from Wyoming were
released into the Long Pines area of southeastern
Montana. Wyoming stock was also used in the Ashland
area of southeastern Montana in 1956 and 1957 when 26
birds were released.*
http://fwp.mt.gov/hunting/planahunt/huntingGuides/turkey/brochure

Lo Mein Noodles with Egg Rolls
4 people ~ tools: high sided frypan
spatula or large serving spoon

16 ounces Chinese style thin egg noodles
1 ounce bag sesame seeds
2 tablespoons teriyaki sauce
4 green onions, cut into one inch pieces
6 ounces bean sprouts
4 cups water
¼ cup olive oil
optional: 1 teaspoon sesame oil added to olive oil
optional: canned chicken or shrimp, can opener

4 Large Frozen Egg Rolls
(the mini egg rolls have very little filling)

AT HOME:
Wrap each egg roll in foil and freeze. Pack in seal tight plastic bags. If they are the mini egg rolls wrap 3 to a foil packet.

Lay egg rolls at the edge of the grill to warm slowly turn occasionally. Pour oil into the bottom of the pan. Pour in noodles and then enough water to cover the noodles. Place on the grill over hot coals and cook until noodles are tender. Add more water if needed. Drain any remaining water. Add a few tablespoons of olive oil to the noodles along with the remaining ingredients. Place fry pan on the grill above medium coals. Move egg rolls onto the grill until hot and crispy.

Butter Chicken Curry
4 people ~ tools: high sided fry pan
spatula or large serving spoon

3 boneless skinless chicken breasts, frozen
2 - 3½ ounce package of Butter Chicken Curry Paste
   we like Kitchens of India brand lots of flavor in a small box
6 tablespoons butter
2½ cups water
vegetable oil
4 large Naan, Focaccia or Flat Bread

Slice each chicken breast lengthwise into 4 thinner pieces so
you would have twelve pieces of chicken.
Pour vegetable oil in the bottom of your fry pan and place on
grill over hot coals. Brown your chicken in the oil and push to
the side of the pan while you add the butter, curry paste and
water. Stir well and pull the chicken back into the sauce.
Cover with aluminum Foil and place Naan on top of the foil to
warm. Move to the side of the grill or over medium low coals
to simmer for 20 minutes or until chicken is done and sauce is
thickened. Serve with Naan or flat bread.

Craving Veggies
4 people ~ tools: 4 squares non stick aluminum foil

2 10 ounce bags frozen Birds Eye® lightly seasoned Asian
       Medley ~ broccoli, carrots, baby corn, sugar snap peas
¾ cup water
Olive oil or margarine
5 ounce foil can of Chow Mein Noodles

Divide the vegetables evenly on the non-stick side of the foil
squares. Sprinkle with water, Drizzle with olive oil and seal
tightly. Place on grill over medium coals for about 20
minutes, turning occasionally. Top with chow mein noodles.

Chicken Quesadilla's
4-8 people ~ tools: heavy aluminum foil, can opener

16 ounce pkg. frozen chicken rotisserie meat pieces
8   large soft corn tortillas
16 ounce pkg. shredded cheddar cheese
2   7 ounce cans chopped green chile's
2   large tomatoes
olive oil
8 squares of aluminum foil a bit larger than the tortilla's

Pour a bit of olive oil on each piece of foil. Put one tortilla on each piece of foil and sweep it around in the oil to fully grease the tortilla. Divide the chicken between the tortilla's and top with cheese, green chilis and tomato. Fold the tortilla in half and wrap the foil around the filled tortilla. Seal the edges and place on the grill over medium coals for 10 to 15 minutes. Turning when needed until both sides are crispy and cheese is melted. *Crush and Pack the chile's can.*

Tacos
4 people ~ tools: fry pan, serving spoon

3 pounds ground beef
1 package taco seasoning
1 package soft corn or flour tortillas'
1 8 ounce package shredded Mexican blend cheese

AT HOME: Cook ground beef and discard water and oil. Add taco seasoning. Pack in quart size plastic freezer bags. Freeze.

IN CAMP: Pour one cup of water into frypan. Add Taco Meat. Heat over medium-hot coals. Place tortillas on top of taco meat to warm, turning once. Sprinkle with cheese. To serve, spoon taco meat onto tortilla and fold in half.

Foil Grilled Potato Nacho's
4 people ~ tools: heavy aluminum foil, can opener

26 ounce bag extra crispy frozen french fries
1 16 oz. can black beans, repackaged in seal tight plastic bag
Can spray canola oil
7 ounce can chopped Green Chiles
16 ounces shredded Mexican blend cheese
Salsa in plastic bottle or my favorite, Valentina Mexican sauce

Spray four squares of foil with oil and divide the potatoes between them. Wrap tight and place on grill over hot coals. Turn often so potatoes crisp but don't burn. Move to the side of the grill and unwrap foil. Spoon on beans and chilies. Return to hot coals until beans are hot. Sprinkle with cheese.

Chicken Foiled Dinner
4 people ~ tools: non-stick heavy aluminum foil, can opener

4 boneless skinless chicken breasts cut in half
6 carrots
4 potatoes
1 onion
1 can cream of chicken soup
1 tablespoon margarine
8 squares heavy aluminum foil

At Home: Boil chicken breast for 20 minutes. Boil carrots and potatoes until they can be pierced with a fork but are still firm. Divide chicken, carrots, potatoes and soup onto four squares of foil. Top with a teaspoon of margarine. Seal tight and wrap in another square of foil. Place in seal tight plastic bag and freeze until needed.

In Camp: Bury in hot coals for 30 minutes, turning twice.

Roasting Hot Sub

4 people ~ tools: sharp knife, heavy aluminum foil, gloves

1 loaf French Bread
2 pounds thinly sliced deli meat
   Mix it up roast beef, chicken, pastrami, what you like
8 ounces sliced pepper jack cheese
8 ounces sliced medium cheddar cheese
2 beefsteak tomatoes
2 large dill pickles
Mayonnaise, Mustard
Canola Oil

Slice bread in half lengthwise. Brush the outside of the bread with oil and place on a long piece of aluminum foil. Spread each piece of bread with mayonnaise. Layer meat, cheese, sliced tomatoes and sliced pickles on the bread with a squeeze of mustard between the layers. Combine both halves of the bread and slice into 4 pieces. Wrap up in the aluminum foil. Place on the grill over medium coals. Turn occasionally. This will take 30 to 40 minutes to heat through, so you may as well enjoy a beer.

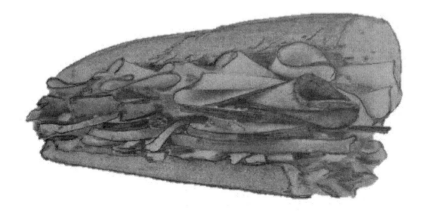

Lazy Boy Bangers and Mash
4 people ~ tools: 1 large frypan, 2 tin coffee cups or saucepan

8 good quality stadium bratwursts
1 family size package dehydrated mashed potatoes
2 cups water (approximately) for cooking potatoes
2 cups water for gravy
½ cup powdered whole milk
1 package homestyle brown gravy mix
4 big slices of butter
cooking oil

Pour a little oil in the bottom of a large frypan with Brats. Place on the grill over hot coals turning the Brats until browned on all sides, about 30 minutes for them to cook through.   Move brats to the side of the grill to keep warm.

Pour 2 cups of water into the frypan and stir in the milk and gravy mix. Continue to stir the gravy until it starts to thicken. Pour gravy into a tin coffee cup and set to the side of the grill to keep warm. Pour 2 cups of water into the frypan and place on the grill until water is not quite boiling. Stir in the mashed potato mix.   Top potatoes with butter and gravy. Serve on tin plates.   Bangers on top or to the side of the potatoes.

Cliff Lake ~ Mission Mountains

Backpackers Alfredo
4 people ~ tools: 1 fry pan with high sides

12 ounces spinach fettuccine
¾ cup butter
4 cups water
½ cup dry whole milk powder
2 cups parmesan cheese, grated
2 tablespoons olive oil
optional: frozen or canned chicken breast meat, can opener

Pour olive oil into the fry pan. Break fettuccine noodles in half and place in fry pan. Pour 3 cups of water into the pan or enough to just cover the fettuccine. Place on grill over hot coals and simmer until noodles are tender. Stir dry powdered milk into one cup of water and mix well. Push the noodles to the sides of the pan so there is a well in the center of the pan. Place the butter in the well to melt, stir the milk in with the butter, stir the cheese into the milk. When the butter is melted and the sauce thoroughly mixed, gently pull the noodles into the alfredo sauce until it is evenly distributed. If adding chicken push noodles to the sides of the pan again, add 2 tablespoons butter to the center of pan, heat the chicken in the butter. Serve when all is warm.

Tangerine Broccoli
4 people ~ tools: high sided fry pan or saucepan

½ bunch fresh broccoli cut into bite size pieces
    or 10-ounce package Frozen Broccoli
4 tangerines
    or a 10 ounce can of mandarin oranges, *can opener*
1 tablespoon butter

Combine broccoli, oranges with juice and butter in pan. Cover with foil and simmer over hot coals until broccoli is tender. *If using frozen broccoli, drain and dry before adding to pan.*

Angel Hair Gorgonzola
4 people ~ tools: fry pan with high sides, fork

1 12 ounces package Angel Hair Pasta
3 cups water
¼ cup olive oil
4 sun dried tomatoes chopped into small pieces
1 ounce package Knorr Spring Dried Vegetables Mix
4 ounces crumbled gorgonzola cheese
serve with Soft Bread Sticks or warm Garlic Bread

Pour ½ the olive oil in the frypan and place on the grill over hot coals. Add the water and stir in the vegetable mix. Bring to a boil. Add a little more water if necessary, you will need enough sauce to cover the pasta. Break the angel hair in half and add to the pan. Angel Hair cooks very quickly so it should only be 5 minutes until it is soft. Don't' overcook or it will be mushy. Drain any excess water. Drizzle the remaining olive oil on the pasta. Gently lift the vegetables to the top of the pan with a fork and sprinkle in the gorgonzola. Serve hot .

Foil Grilled Tomato & Zucchini
4 people ~ tools: 4 squares heavy aluminum foil

2 medium size zucchinis scrubbed or peeled
4 large roma tomatoes, *I use roma's because they pack better*
2 tablespoons butter or margarine
salt and pepper

Slice zucchini and tomatoes onto the foil, divided equally. Salt and pepper as desired, top with butter. Fold up tightly but leave a little opening for steam to escape. Place on the grill over hot coals for about 10 minutes on each side.

Pastrami Carbonara

4 to 6 people ~ tools: high sided fry pan, fork

4 cups water
4 tablespoons olive oil
16 ounce package thin spaghetti
16 ounces deli pastrami, chopped
8 ounces cream cheese
Soft Bread Sticks or warm Garlic Bread packaged in foil

At Home: Chop pastrami and freeze in quart size freezer bag.

In Camp: Bring water and 2 tablespoons of oil to a boil over hot coals or low flame. Place foiled package of cream cheese to the side of the grill to soften.

Break spaghetti in half and add to boiling water. Cook until spaghetti is tender. Drain any remaining water. Immediately stir in two tablespoons oil and pastrami. When pastrami is hot stir in the softened cream cheese. Don't wait … Enjoy now!

Parmesan Asparagus

4 people ~ tools: heavy aluminum foil

1½ pounds fresh asparagus
2 teaspoons olive oil
1 teaspoon lemon pepper
1 cup dried grated parmesan cheese
¼ to ½ cup of water

Trim hard ends of asparagus and place on 12 x 20 inch sheet of heavy aluminum foil. Drizzle with oil, sprinkle with plenty of lemon pepper and parmesan. Sprinkle with water and wrap your foil tightly around the asparagus package.

Place on grill over hot coals for about 20 minutes or until asparagus is tender. Turn once or twice.

Backpackers Red Spaghetti

4 people ~ tools: 1 large cook pot or high side fry pan

16 ounces frozen meat balls
2 packages Spaghetti Sauce Mix
2 cups water
2 six ounce cans low sodium V8® Vegetable Juice
1 8 ounce package thin spaghetti
2 tablespoons margarine or vegetable oil
Garlic Bread packaged in foil

Put vegetable oil and meatballs in the cook pot on the grill over hot coals. Brown lightly. Push meatball to the outside edges of the pan. Add water to the center of the pan and stir in sauce mix until it dissolves. Add V8 juice and heat until liquid starts to simmer. Break spaghetti in half and add to liquid. Simmer until spaghetti is tender. About 8 minutes.

Note: The V8 cans provide more water and are lighter and easier to crush than can tomato sauce. Crush cans and Pack them out in the seal tight plastic bag you brought for garbage.

Baby Corn on the Cob with mixed vegetables

4 people ~ tools: heavy aluminum foil

1 15 ounce can whole baby corn
1 10 ounce bag frozen mixed vegetables
4 Tablespoons butter
salt and pepper

At home, repackage corn into a quart size seal tight plastic bag. In camp combine corn and vegetables on an 18-inch length of aluminum foil. Salt and Pepper to taste. Top with butter or margarine and seal well. Place on grill over hot coals for 20 minutes, turning occasionally.

The Mighty Dog Cook Off

This is a group recipe in which each member of your group brings a surprise ingredient to make your dog taste even more delicious. Of course, there is the "got to have it" mustard and pickles, but other favorites include chili and cheese, sauerkraut, swiss cheese, mushroom and onion, and of course, Everything's Better With Bacon.

Bacon Wrapped Dog
8 people ~ tools: wood toothpicks

1 package of 8 all beef wieners
8 ounces bacon
3 large slicing tomatoes, sliced
1 red onion, sliced
1 jar Pico de Gallo sauce
Pkg of 8 hot dog buns

Wrap bacon around each weiner and secure with a toothpick. Place on the grill about eight inches above medium hot coals. Turn often to avoid burning your bacon. Grill until bacon is crisp. Serve on buns with tomatoes, onion and sauce.

Chili Dog

8 people: large cook pot, paper bowls, knives and forks
can opener, serving spoon

8 ballpark franks
2 28-ounce cans chili ~ repackaged into seal tight bags
1 16-ounce package of finely shredded cheddar cheese
1 large sweet onion, diced
yellow mustard
8 potato rolls

Heat the canned chili in the cookpot on the grill over medium coals. Stir often to not burn the bottom. Move pot to the side and grill the franks. Split the rolls in half and put in the bottom of each bowl. Top with grilled franks, lots of chili, cheese, onion and mustard

Beer Brats & Kraut

Frankfurters, Sauerkraut and bacon all grilled together
8 people ~ tools: aluminum foil

1   package of 8 Brats
16 ounce sauerkraut, packaged *in plastic.*
4   dill pickles sliced lengthwise
3   Tablespoons dried minced onion
8   hero rolls, split but not all the way through
squeeze bottle of margarine
spicy brown mustard

Slice franks lengthwise but not all the way through. Stuff each frank with pickle slices, sauerkraut, and onion. Wrap two bacon slices around each frank to hold in the stuffing. Wrap stuffed dog in foil. Place on grill about eight inches above hot coals, turning often. Grill about 20 minutes or until bacon is brown and crispy. Toast the outside of your hero roll for a minute with a squeeze of margarine before serving.

Packing Light Desserts

Apples n Fudge Fondue
*4 people ~ tools: 4 pack of aluminum foil mini loaf pans,
can opener*

4 large Apples
1 12 ounce package semi-sweet chocolate chips
2 cups mini marshmallows
1 small can, 8 ounces, condensed milk
5 tablespoons butter

Divide the butter and milk into the foil pans and place on grill
to melt over low coals. Stir in chocolate chips and
marshmallows. Continue to stir until chocolate and
marshmallows are melted. Dip sliced apples in warm
chocolate. Mmmm!
Even easier: dip sliced apples in Caramel Ice Cream Sauce

Wild Berry Pudding
*2 to 4 people ~ tools: wide mouth beverage container, coffee
cups*

1 package instant lemon pudding mix
1 cup dry whole milk powder
2 cups water
2 cup fresh berries
Optional: granola or chopped pecans

Pour water into a 4 cup wide mouth beverage container with a
screw top lid. Add milk powder and pudding mix. Cover and
shake vigorously for one minute. Pour into coffee cups and
stir in berries. Cover and allow to set for 10 minutes.
Sprinkle top with granola or chopped nuts.

Hot Baked Fruit
6 people ~ 8x8 square aluminum foil cake pan, can opener

6 ounces pitted prunes
6 ounces dried apricots
6 ounce can pineapple chunks, undrained
15 ounce can cherry pie filling
   repackaged into a quart size seal tight plastic bag
½ cup walnut pieces
¼ cup margarine
Biscotti or Shortbread

Grease the bottom of the cake pan with margarine. Mix everything into the cake pan, including the pineapple juice. Place on the grill over medium low coals stirring every few minutes until the liquid is absorbed into the fruit. Serve with biscotti or shortbread

Limoncello & Berries Cake
2 to 4 people ~ tools: a wide mouth coffee cup per person

2 one ounce bottles of Limoncello Liquor
1 pint fresh raspberries or sliced strawberries
1 small lemon flavored pound cake

Divide berries equally among cups. Pour Limoncello onto the berries and allow to sit for about 30 minutes until the berry juice starts to mix with the liquor. Cut cake into bite size pieces and add to berries. With a fork gently mix cake into the fruit.

Mountain Fudge

16 ounce carton Chocolate Fudge Frosting
1 cup chopped walnuts. Optional: craisins mini marshmallows
Stir nuts, craisins, marshmallows into frosting.

Huckleberry Danish
4 people ~ tools: 4 12 inch squares non-stick aluminum foil

4 Large Cream Cheese Danish Rolls
¼ pound butter ~ *preferably Amish roll butter*
1 8 ounce package softened cream cheese spread
1 4 ounce jar huckleberry jam

Place one Danish (cream side down) on each square of foil. Place on the grill over medium hot coals one to two minutes until lightly toasted. Flip Danish over and dot with butter slices. Spread cream cheese on each roll and place a tablespoon of jam on each roll. Wrap up the foil but leave a small opening in the top for steam to escape. Heat on the grill over low coals until butter and jam melt. Careful not to burn.

Nutella Cheesecake Quesadilla
4 people ~ tools: 4 12 inch squares non-stick aluminum foil

1 8 ounce jar Nutella Hazelnut Spread
1 8 ounce package cream cheese
8 inch flour tortilla's
8-12 strawberries, sliced or one pint fresh raspberries'

Spread Nutella on one half of each tortilla and cream cheese on the other half. Spread sliced strawberries over the Nutella half and fold over.   Wrap in foil and place on grill over hot coals for about 3 minutes, flip and heat the other side.
If you don't have non-stick foil, spray the outside of the tortilla with olive or canola oil.

S'mores Dip
2-4 people ~ tools: non-stick aluminum foil

Fashion a flat bowl out of a doubled piece of foil. Place one tablespoon of margarine on the foil and top with 1 cup each of sliced strawberries, mini marshmallows and chocolate chips. Turn up the sides of the foil and place on grill over medium coals until melted. Dip Graham Crackers into the melted mix.

Raspberry Nectarines

4 people~ tools: 8x8 square aluminum foil cake pan, serving spoon

4 Firm Nectarines
8 ounces fresh raspberries
3 tablespoons butter or margarine (not water added margarine)
Optional: strawberry shortcake bread
 shake can whip cream

Put 8 slices of butter in foil cake pan. Slice each nectarine off the pit into 8 pieces and place on top of butter slice. Place the cake pan on the grill over medium hot coals. When the nectarine starts to sizzle in the butter toss in the raspberries. Serve when hot.
Note: Butter is Best!! But it burns easily, so watch closely.

Cinnamon Rolls on a Stick

8 people ~ tools: sharpened willow sticks

1 package of 8 refrigerated cinnamon rolls
¼ pound butter
1 jar of orange marmalade

Carefully wrap one cinnamon roll around one willow stick. Pinch the end to seal the dough around the stick. Bake high over hot coals, like a marshmallow, until the dough is lightly browned and firm. Pull off the stick and fill the center with butter & marmalade.

Extra Dark Hot Chocolate
Good because you control the amount of sugar and create an extra dark chocolate treat

2 cups powdered whole milk
1 cup unsweetened cocoa powder, *like Hersheys*
1 cup non-dairy creamer
½ cup powdered sugar
1 bag mini marshmallows or spray on whipping cream

At Home:
Mix all ingredients except marshmallows in a seal tight plastic bag.

In Camp:
Fill coffee pot with water and bring to a boil over hot coals. Pour water into coffee cups and stir in 3 or more tablespoons of cocoa mix. Top with marshmallows.

Russian Tea Mix

½ cup powdered iced tea mix
1 cup powdered orange drink mix ~ *like Tang*
2 tablespoons powdered lemonade mix ~ like crystal light
½ teaspoon ground allspice
½ teaspoon ground cinnamon

At Home:
Mix all ingredients in
a seal tight plastic bag.

In Camp:
Fill coffee pot with water and
 bring to a boil over hot coals.

Pour into coffee cup and stir in 2 to 3 tablespoons tea mix.

RIVERS AND RAFTS
Stream Access

RIVER ACCESS is an emotional issue in Montana. The Stream Access law currently provides us the opportunity to use our rivers to the high water mark. It is extremely important that each of us remain courteous of the landowners and not infringe on their privacy or their property. In many instances it is the property owner who is maintaining the road that gets you where you want to go. Take time to know the country you are floating walking or driving through. If you are floating through private land stop only where you have room below the ordinary high water mark and then only if necessary.   If you plan to camp make sure you are on public land or you have permission from the **property owner**, not a friend, cousin or brother. Don't assume a prior permission is good for another time or person.

The continuation of our right to navigate Montana's waters is the responsibility of all of us. Let us ensure that right for our children and grandchildren by maintaining respect for the land and its caretakers

"STREAM ACCESS IN MONTANA RIGHTS AND RESPONSIBLITIES OF LANDOWNERS AND RECREATIONISTS. This brochure summarizes the ways in which Montana's 1985 stream access law affects the recreational use of the state's rivers and streams and incorporates the ways the law has been interpreted by the courts in Montana."

Detailed maps of fishing access sites, legal camping on several prominent Montana rivers can be found by accessing Montana.Gov Fish wildlife and Parks: map of Montana Rivers.

http://fwp.mt.gov/fish/guide/fasGuide.html

History and Details of Stream Access

Wickepedia

"The core law creating the Montana Stream Access law began with Article IX, section 3 of the 1972 Montana Constitution, which addressed state ownership of Montana waters. In 1984 in *Montana Coalition for Stream Access, Inc. v. Curran,* the Montana Supreme Court held that "under the public trust doctrine and the 1972 Montana Constitution, any surface waters that are capable of recreational use may be so used by the public without regard to streambed ownership or navigability for nonrecreational purposes."[4] This decision was expanded upon in the same year by *Mont. Coalition for Stream Access, Inc. v. Hildreth*.[5] Both cases noted that streambed access did not imply that the public had a right to cross private lands to access streams.[6] Following *Curran* and *Hildreth*, the Montana Legislature enacted the Stream Access Law in 1985.[6] "

The law creates two classifications of waters capable of recreational use: Class I and Class II.

Class I are waters which are capable of recreational use and have been declared navigable or which are capable of specific kinds of commercial activity including commercial outfitting with multi-person watercraft. Class II waters are all other rivers and streams capable of recreational use that are not Class I waters.[2]"

"NATIONAL PARKS, INDIAN RESERVATIONS AND WILDLIFE REFUGES, may have special rules.

On February 10, 1977, Governor Thomas Judge signed the law designating the Blackspotted Cutthroat Trout as Montana's official state fish. Mt.gov

Montana has the rare distinction of being the headwaters of three major watersheds where two continental divides intersect at **Triple Divide Peak** in Glacier National Park. The Laurentian Divide and the Continental Divide.

On the northeast side of Triple Divide Peak water flows into the Saint Mary's River that joins the Saskatchewan River Basin and eventually empties into Hudson Bay.

Water west of the divide flows into the Flathead River which empties into the Clark Fork that joins the Columbia River to the Pacific Ocean.

Water south east of the divide feeds the Marias River that joins the Missouri River then the Mississippi River that empties into the Gulf of Mexico.

West of the Continental Divide the Clark Fork river flows northwest from Butte to Missoula where it is joined by the Blackfoot River, the Bitterroot River and the Flathead River before entering Idaho near Lake Pend Oreille.

 The Kootenai River flows north through Canada and is a major contributor to the Columbia River at Castlegar.

East of the Continental Divide the Gallatin River, the Madison River and the Jefferson River join at Three Forks to become the Missouri River.

The Yellowstone River runs freely, undammed for 670 miles from its headwaters in Yellowstone Park where it joins the Missouri River in North Dakota.

The Rivers Map

I once belonged to a **Float of the Month Club.** I admit the January and February Floats were canceled due to ice but we floated the **Beaverhead** in March. I have never been so cold as on the Beaverhead. The wind was blowing us upriver faster than a person could walk. Other than a couple of fishing access sites the Beaverhead is almost all privately owned so we could not get out and walk. It also winds back on itself over and over so what appeared to be a half day float turned into an eight hour struggle with the wind and hypothermia.

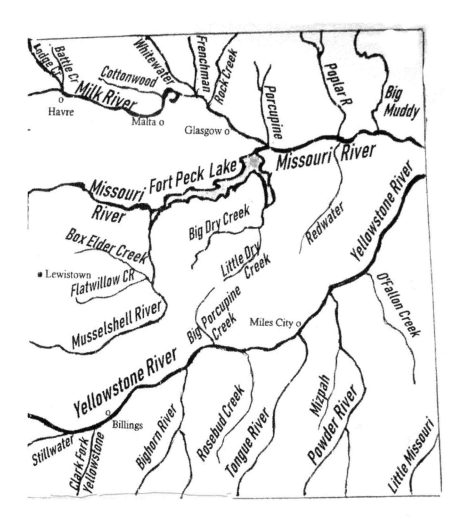

DON'T FORGET YOUR OARS

Ice on **The Madison** was just breaking up in April but it was a great float. Except one of our group of two boats arrived at camp without oars and had to drive back to Helena before we could depart. We floated **The Smith** that year in May. It was the year before they Implemented the DRAW for a permit to float. Seriously, there were times on the river when you could literally walk across the river on rafts. Campsites were full and filthy from overuse. In my opinion the permit system for The Smith is a good thing.

Class I Waters

West of the Continental Divide

Kootenai River Drainage:
Kootenai River - from Libby Dam to the Idaho border
Lake Creek - from the Chase cut-off road to its
    confluence with the Kootenai River

Yaak River:
    from Yaak Falls to its confluence with the Kootenai River

Flathead River Drainage:
South Fork of the Flathead -
    from Youngs Creek to Hungry Horse Reservoir
Middle Fork of the Flathead -
    from Schaffer Creek to its confluence with the mainstem
    of the Flathead River
Flathead River (mainstem) - to its confluence with the
    Clark Fork of the Columbia River

Clark Fork River Drainage:
    from Warm Spring Creek to the Idaho border

North Fork of the Blackfoot:
    from Highway 200 east of Ovando to its confluence with
    the mainstem of the Blackfoot Riiver

Blackfoot River:
    from the Cedar Meadow fishing Access Site west of
    Helmville to its confluence with the Clark Fork

Bitterroot River:
    from the confluence of the East and West forks to its
    confluence with the Clark Fork

Rock Creek:
    from the confluence of the West Fork to its confluence
    with the Clark Fork

East of the Continental Divide

Missouri River Drainage:

Big Hole River ~ from Fishtrap Fishing Access Site
   downstream from Wisdom to its confluence with the
   Beaverhead River at Twin Bridges
Beaverhead River ~ from Clark Canyon Dam to its confluence
   with the Big Hole at Twin Bridges
Jefferson River ~ from Twin Bridges to its confluence with the
   Missouri at Three Forks
Madison River ~ from Quake Lake to its confluence with the
   Missouri at Three Forks
Gallatin River ~ from Taylors Fork to its confluence with the
   Missouri at Three Forks
Missouri River ~ from Three Forks to the North Dakota border

Dearborn River ~ from the Highway 434 bridge to its
   confluence with the Missouri at Dearborn
Sun River (also called the Medicine River) ~ from Gibson Dam
   to its confluence with the Missouri at Great Falls
Smith River ~ from Camp Baker Fishing Access Site near
   Fort Logan to its confluence with the Missouri near Ulm
Marias River ~ from Tiber Dam to its confluence with the
   Missouri near Loma
Judith River ~ from the confluence of Big Spring Creek to its
   confluence with the Missouri near Judith Landing

Yellowstone River Drainage:

Yellowstone River ~ flows through Gardiner from Yellowstone
   National Park to the North Dakota border
Bighorn River ~ from Yellowtail Dam to its confluence with
   the Yellowstone near Hysham
Tongue River ~ from Tongue River Dam to its confluence
   with the Yellowstone at Miles City

Rivers and Rafts

Packing List for a Raft Trip

BOAT BAG	
	Collapsible water bucket
	Grill, wrapped in garbage bag
	Tent (two to four man)
	First aid kit
	Water purifier, filter
	Roll top table
	Biodegradable soap & scrubber sponge in a ziplock bag
	Boat repair kit
	Duct tape
	Rescue ropes
	Small saw, axe and shovel
	Briquettes
	Portable gas grill and fuel
	Cooking Water and Drinking Water a gallon per day per person
	Tarp for under your tent
	Tarp and rope for a rain shelter. Clothesline rope works well, Parachute rope is stronger
	Portable toilet if required
	Maps that show River Access, School Trust Land, Public and Private Land: montana.gov river access maps
Your Additions:	

COOK BAG	
	Coffee pot, insulated stainless steel french press
	Fry pan with high sides, sheet pan
	Cook pot
	Cake pan
	Heavy aluminum foil
	Gallon size seal tight plastic bags for garbage
	Wood matches & wax paper packed in zip lock bag
	Leather gloves for cooking & wood
	Dish washing tub: packed with plates & silverware
	Tin plates, Paper plates, Sharp knife, forks & spoons
	Serving spoon and Spatula, Can opener, Cork screw
	Coffee cups are also soup bowls
	2 large flour sack dish towels
	Wine or drink glasses wrapped in dish towels
	Plastic Table Cloth for ground cover and food prep
	First Aid minimum: Neosporin, Skin Tape, Aspirin, Bandaid Liquid Antseptic, Baking Soda Toothpaste and chewable baby aspirin for bee stings in the mouth
Your additions:	

DRY BOX

Easy to pack rubber lock top boxes *14x20x12 is just the right size*, one will hold your kitchen and another will hold your dry foods

	Coffee, cocoa, powdered Gatorade
	Salt & pepper
	Peanut Butter and Jelly
	Catsup, Mustard, Worcestershire Sauce
	Canola Oil
	Licorice, energy bars, peanuts, snack mix

COOLER

	Freeze Water in Milk Jugs for drinking and cooking
	Soda, Beer, Wine
	Milk, Coffee Cream, Butter, Mayonnaise
	Eggs
	Meat
	Cheese

Your additions:

WHAT TO WEAR	
	Layer Tank top, T Shirt and Polar Fleece sweater
	Lightweight quick dry pants or shorts
	Water Sandals
	Sunglasses
	Don't forget
	Folding Camp Chair
	Fishing license
	Fishing Rod, Waders, Vest, Flies or lures. Bait fishing is illegal on many streams. Check the rules.
MY WATER BAG	
	Water socks if its cold water, 1 or 2 pair of socks for cold feet night or day
	Light weight sweatpants double as jammies if you are sharing a tent
	Shorts, Canvas Camp Pants
	Hiking shoes, Camp slippers are nice if you have room.
	Rain Gear, Hat and gloves
	Toothbrush, Baking Soda toothpaste, Floss, Comb, Eye drops, Biodegradable Shampoo (doubles as body wash) Mirror *car visor mirrors are a good size,* Washcloth.... *awesome with hot water from the coffee pot.*
	Flexible bandaids, chewable baby aspirin, ibuprofen
	Sunscreen and lip sunscreen, bug repellent *I prefer lemon grass essential oil to repel insects*
	Sleeping bag and self-inflating sleeping pad
	Fleece Jacket also works as a pillow. *A pillowcase for your fleece is nice*
Your additions:	

Lazy Boy Shop and Go River Menu

Four people on the river three days
Tools: 8 cup coffee pot, camp grill, high sided frypan, leather cook gloves, matches, plates, silverware, spatula, heavy aluminum foil, seal tight plastic bags both quart and gallon size (don't buy the zipper bags, they do not seal tight). For a better cup of coffee bring an insulated French Press and use your regular coffee pot for boiling water.

Breakfast
Coarse Ground Coffee (if you aren't using a filter)
cream, sugar, cocoa, juice

1 box of instant pancake mix (the add water only kind)
1 large ham steak, maple syrup

12 eggs, 12 oz. package grated cheddar cheese,
16 ounce package fully cooked sausage links, 8 tortillas, salsa

8 english muffins, Butter, Peanut Butter
Old Fashioned Oatmeal or Steel Cut Oats, chopped dried fruit

Dinner One
2 pounds Hamburger, 8 pack english muffins or burger buns
cheese, pickles, catsup
1 24oz bag tater tots
aluminum foil

Dinner Two
4 steaks, size of your choice
1 24 oz bag ravioli
2 onions
1 pkg sliced mushrooms
3 tomatoes
olive oil

Royal Wulff

Dinner Three
6 -8 polish sausage's
6-8 hero sandwich buns
1 jar dill pickles sliced lengthwise, mustard

Lunch
1 pound sliced deli turkey
1 pound sliced deli ham
1 pound sliced deli roast beef or pastrami
12 ounce package sliced swiss cheese
12 ounce package sliced cheddar cheese
Package of 12 tortillas for wraps

Condiments
Salt, pepper, salsa, catsup, steak sauce, mustard,
mayonnaise, butter

Beverages
WATER! One gallon per person/per day should be enough to
include coffee & cocoa, powdered energy drinks and limited
cooking. Soda, Juice, Beer, Wine, Liquor

Deserts
Large bag mini candy bars
Box of favorite cookies
Licorice

At home preparation:
Keep your food out of the ice water. Fill clean plastic milk or
juice jugs with water and freeze for the food cooler.

Hamburger: Pack in seal tight plastic bags and freeze.

Tater Tots: divide onto 2 large squares of aluminum foil.
Wrap and seal edges, Pack in Gallon size seal tight bag,
freeze.

Steak: Tenderize, season and pack in freezer bags. Freeze

Ravioli: Divide ravioli on two squares of aluminum foil. Top
with sliced mushrooms, chopped tomato, chopped onion,
season with garlic, salt, pepper and margarine slices. Wrap
and seal edges, freeze.

Make it Easy River Menu

4 people 4 day Menu

Page	Breakfast
97	Hero Eggs
98	Merry Dave McMuffins
95	Breakfast in a Boat
157	Fruit Fried Oats
	Lunch, Snacks Appetizers
108	Nancy's River Sandwich
106	Stromboli Wrap
106	Rosebud Ham and Apple Pita
	Chinese Pork, Spicy Brown Mustard
	Dinner
128,129	Steak on a Stick, New Potatoes
123	Creole Rice
124	Pork Chops and Beans
139	Crazy Mountain Hash
	Dessert
146	Banana Nut Croissants
147	Cherry Cheesecake
148	Big Horn Rice Pudding
148	Irish Coffee

How to open a bottle of wine without a cork screw

You will need a shoe with a firm sole. A river sandal should work nicely. Hold the bottle of wine at an upside down angle in one hand and the the toe of the shoe in the other hand. Tap firmly on the bottom of the wine bottle until the cork moves out far enough for you to grip with your fingers.

Black Tie Supper for 12

A memorable meal deserves a tablecloth. Dress to Impress!

Tools ~ plastic cocktail glasses, forks can opener	**Shrimp Cocktail** 4 4 ounces cans medium shrimp 2 jars spicy cocktail sauce 2 stalks celery, diced 3 Lemons, Lemon pepper
Page 127 Tools ~ 12 sharpened green willow branches or wood skewers sharp knife, cutting board	**Steak on a Stick** 8 pounds Tenderloin Steaks 1 bottle Worcestershire Sauce 1 pound bacon spray canola oil Webers® Steak & Chop seasoning meat tenderizer steak sauce
Page 128 Tools ~ aluminum foil turkey pan, Serving spoon can opener sturdy paper plates, forks, aluminum foil	**New Potatoes and Button Mushrooms** 10 pound bag mixed new potatoes 2 pounds fresh button mushrooms 2 tablespoon olive oil 1 pound real butter ~ not margarine Salt and Pepper 3 cups fresh water
Page 209 stainless steel mixing bowl hand beater paper plates liqueur glasses	**Huckleberry Crepes & Grand Marnier** 12 to 16 pre-made crepes 1 12 oz jar Huckleberry Jam 2 pounds frozen huckleberries or blueberries 16 oz. heavy whipping cream 2 tsp. sugar Tip: Serve the Marnier in liqueur glasses pass the bowl of whipping cream around the table so everyone takes a turn at whipping the cream.

Rivers and Rafts Breakfast

No Time Coffee & No Time Breakfast

I love my morning coffee and seriously, there was a time on the Smith River that there was no time for coffee. If you weren't the first boat on the water, you were not catching fish. In the final years, before you needed a permit to float, I remember a trip there were so many boats on the water it was hard to find room to oar. Finding a camp was first come or you got lucky and someone was willing to move over and share their spot.

Mikes Fix: Chocolate Covered Coffee Beans. Yumm!
Even better, mix with raisins and peanuts, enjoy fishing.

No Time Breakfast

One: 1 cup Frosted Mini Wheats
½ cup dried cherries or strawberries
½ cup raisins
½ cup walnuts
Combine in a seal tight plastic bag
Enjoy with Orange Juice Box

Two: Peanut Butter Croissants
3 people: tools: Slicing knife

3 large bakery Croissants
1 jar extra crunchy peanut butter
1 jar Huckleberry Jam
Enjoy with 3 cartons Chocolate Milk

Breakfast in A Boat
3 people: tools ~ Slicing knife, cutting board

3 slices Pita Bread
6 precooked shelled hardboiled eggs
from the refrigerator isle
16 ounce package diced cooked ham
3 large slicing Tomatoes
6 thick slices of soft goat cheese
Durkees® Dressing, and/or mayonnaise & mustard, pepper
3 cans V-8 juice, can opener if needed

Slice Pita Bread in half and open the center, spread the inside with Durkees®. Thinly slice Eggs and Tomato. Pepper the eggs and tomato. Stuff the Pita halves with eggs, tomato, and cheese. Enjoy with a can of V-8

Egg Salad Sandwich
3 people ~ tools: Slicing knife

3 large bakery Croissants
6 hard-boiled eggs
3 tablespoons real mayonnaise
1 teaspoon Durkees® Dressing or mustard
½ cup diced celery
Salt and Pepper
Serve with applesauce cups.

At Home: Submerge eggs in a pan of cold water so they are in a single layer and bring to a boil. Remove from the heat and let stand for 15 minutes. Drain the water and fill pan with ice water. Peel cold eggs. Chop eggs and mix in mayonnaise, Durkees, Celery, salt and pepper. Pack in seal tight bag. Keep refrigerated at home. Keep cold in the cooler up to three days. Do not leave out of cooler longer than one hour. Spread on Croissants.

Fruit Wrap
Carrie Lee, Missoula Montana

1 whole wheat tortilla per person
apple slices
banana slices
peanut butter
honey

The beauty of the fruit wrap is you can use any fruit that you have available on your trip. Carrie spreads a thin layer of peanut butter on her tortilla first. Then slices an apple, banana, or other fruit such as peaches or pears. Top it off with a squeeze of honey.

Hero Eggs

4 people ~ tools: aluminum foil, serving spoon

6 prepared hard boiled eggs from the dairy isle
2 Tablespoons mayonnaise
1 Tablespoon mustard
Black pepper
16 ounce package of diced cooked ham
4 green onions chopped
1 green pepper chopped
1 large dill pickle chopped

4 long hero buns or hot dog buns
4 squares aluminum foil
2 tablespoons butter or margarine
sliced cheese: optional
spray canola oil

At Home:
Slice eggs into a mixing bowl and stir in mayonnaise and mustard, sprinkle with black pepper. Place chopped ham on a paper towel to absorb moisture. Add ham, onion, pepper and pickles to the eggs and mix lightly. Spoon into a quart size seal tight plastic bag. Keep refrigerated.

In Camp:
Spray the outside of each bun with oil and place on a square of aluminum foil. Butter the inside of your bun. Place a slice of cheese inside then top with ham & egg mix. Wrap in foil and heat over medium coals. Turn occasionally. Serve in foil.

These can be heated while you are packing the boat as long as you don't forget to turn the sandwiches and they burn. You will be a hero handing out hot sandwiches to everyone on the boat.

Butter Cream Eggs

4 people ~ tools: 1 high sided fry pan or sheet pan, spatula, mixing bowl, tin cup or small cook pot, fork, patience 😊

8 eggs
8 ounces cream cheese
4 tablespoons butter
Salt and Pepper
4 Croissants wrapped in aluminum foil

Combine 4 tablespoons butter with cream cheese in a tin cup and place on the grill over low coals. When butter is melted stir well and set aside.

Crack eggs into a mixing bowl, add a little salt and pepper and beat well with fork or old style hand mixer. Mix in cream cheese and butter.

Place 2 tablespoons butter in a fry pan and place on the grill over medium low coals. Spread melted butter around the pan and pour in egg mix. Cook slowly. Gently turn eggs occasionally, until cooked through. Serve on warm croissants.

Basketball

+

InnerTube

=

River Ball

100

Merry Dave McMuffins

4 people: tools: 1 fry pan, spatula, tin plate, aluminum foil
Recipe is for 4 people but Dave often cooks for 20 or more.
A large griddle works best for a crowd.

4 English Muffins
4 Tablespoons butter or margarine
4 slices ham
4 eggs
salt & pepper
4 slices swiss cheese
4 slices cheddar cheese
Durkees® Dressing

Split muffins in half and spread margarine on the muffins.
Place 4 halves into fry pan, margarine side down, and toast
briefly over medium hot coals. Stack on a tin plate and cover
with foil. Move to the side of the grill to keep warm. Toast the
other 4 muffins halves and move to the plate.

Arrange 4 ham slices in the fry pan separately without
stacking them. Heat and flip the ham. Crack one egg on each
slice of ham, sunny side up style.

Cover with the aluminum foil from the toast. Spread
Durkees® on both sides of each muffin. When egg whites are
well cooked, top with cheese, cover again and allow cheese
to melt slightly. Lift ham, egg and cheese stack with a
spatula onto each muffin, top with another muffin half to serve
sandwich style.

Dave's Hopper

Wooley Bugger

Big Hole Boiled Omelet

tools: 1 deep cook pot, tongs, leather gloves

2 eggs per person
1 quart size seal tight freezer bags for each 2 eggs
salt and pepper or other seasoning
Omelet ingredients of your choice
may include fully cooked diced ham, shredded cheddar
cheese, pepper jack cheese, chopped onion, bell peppers,
sliced mushrooms, sliced black olives

Drop a few little rocks into the bottom of the cook pot. Fill the
pot ¾ full with water and bring to a boil over hot coals.

Crack 2 eggs into a quart size seal tight plastic bag. Seal and
squish the eggs to mix. Open the bag and add any other
omelet ingredients you wish. Squish some more, tightly seal
the bag and drop into the pot of boiling water. The rocks
should keep the bag from touching the bottom of the pan. It
should float freely and not touch sides of the cook pot either.
Boil 8 to 10 minutes or until your eggs look done. Remove
with tongs and leather gloves being careful not to pierce the
zip lock bag. *You really do not want to lose your omelet in the
water.* You can eat this from the bag but it will be very hot so
put the bag on a plate.   *Thanks Cheryl Woolverton, Butte MT*

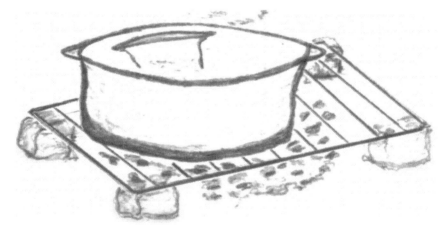

Trout Benedict

4 people ~ tools: 1 fry pan, 1 small saucepot, spatula, tin plate
*   aluminum foil*

1 large fresh caught trout or 2 smaller trout
8 eggs sunny side up
4 buttermilk biscuits
1 package Hollandaise sauce mix
2 tablespoons butter
½ cup coffee cream
½ cup water
lemon pepper
olive oil

Clean trout, poach in ½ cup water over medium coals until flakey. Discard skin and bones. Flake the trout with a fork and sprinkle with lemon pepper . Transfer to a clean tin plate.

Put water In the small sauce pot and stir in hollandaise sauce mix add butter and cream. Heat over low coals until bubbly, stirring often, set aside.

Wipe fry pan of fish residue and drizzle olive oil into the pan. Crack eggs into the pan without breaking the yolk and cook until the whites are cooked and yokes are runny.

Split the biscuits and slide a half biscuit under each egg. Top with flaked fish. Cover with foil and return to low heat until biscuits are warm. Serve with a spoonful of hot hollandaise on each biscuit.

Note: "Sunny Side Up" is a term used when you want the whites of your eggs cooked but the yoke runny. "Over Easy" is a term used when you want your eggs turned once, trying not to break the egg yolk, and served with a soft cooked center.

Breakfast Taco

4 -8 people ~ tools: 1 fry pan, spatula, non-stick alluminum foil, paper plates, forks

8 soft corn tortilla's
8 eggs
16 fully cooked sausage links, cut into small pieces
12 ounces frozen tater tots
12 ounces shredded Mexican cheese
8 ounce bottle mild taco sauce or salsa
canola oil, salt, pepper

Place grill about 8 inches above hot coals. Wrap tortilla's in foil and place on the side of the grill to warm. Line pan with foil. Smash tater tots in the pan with a fork, add sausage pieces and place on the grill. When potatoes are browned flip once to brown the other side. Push potatoes to one side of the pan and drizzle oil onto the other side of the pan. Crack eggs into the oil and scramble. Season with salt and pepper.

Assemble tacos ~ top with cheese and taco sauce.

Fried Rainbow Trout with Lemon Butter

4 people ~ tools: 1 baking sheet, saucepan, spatula, tin plate, aluminum foil

2 – 3 trout depending on size
6 lemons
6 tablespoons butter (not margarine)
Salt and Pepper
Crisco hard vegetable shortening, *if you like a crispy skin*

Remove the heads from fresh cleaned trout. If the trout is still wet damp dry it with a paper towel. Place the trout skin side down on a greased foil lined baking sheet, *you can use a frypan also but it's not as easy.* Generously Salt and Pepper both the inside and the outside of the trout. Squeeze the juice of two lemons up and down the meat inside the fish. Place the baking sheet on a grill about 5 inches over hot coals. Cook for 5 to 10 minutes per side or until the meat flakes when tested with a fork.

While your trout is cooking. Heat butter in the saucepan over medium coals and stir in the juice of two lemons. Continue to stir until butter is melted then remove from heat.

When fish is flaky and cooked through open the fish flat and pull the spine bones out slowly, starting at the neck and moving down to the tail.

Divide fish onto warmed tin plates and spoon hot lemon butter over the top. Serve with the remaining two lemons cut into wedges.

Note: there could be a few bones remaining so caution those eating to check for bones before swallowing.

Shake Em Up Eggs

4 people ~ tools: fry pan or griddle, spatual, can opener

6 eggs
1 medium tomato
1 cup shredded cheddar cheese
2 cans sliced new potatoes (15 ounces each)
Dash of salt and pepper
1 tablespoon margarine ~ not low fat or softened
1 tablespoon canola oil

At Home: Freeze a small wide mouth insulated water bottle. Crack eggs into the bottle, refrigerate until you are ready to put into the cooler.

In Camp:
Open cans of potatoes and drain all liquid. Melt margarine with oil in fry pan over medium coals. Tilt the pan to coat with melted margarine. Pour potatoes into hot skillet. Chop tomato and add to eggs along with shredded cheese, salt and pepper. Screw lid onto the bottle and shake it up. Flip potatoes and pour eggs onto fried potatoes.

Serve with fish on a stick or sausage links on a stick.

Fried Biscuits with Sausage Gravy

4-6 people ~ tools: Fry pan with high sides, spatula, bowl or plastic bag, aluminum foil, paper towels

1 8 ounce package of complete biscuit mix
Water ~ a little less than package directions for a drier biscuit
1 pinch salt
1 Tbsp canola oil

Combine biscuit mix, salt, and water in plastic bag and squish together until well mixed. Heat oil in the pan over medium coals.   Pull tablespoon size chunks of biscuit mix out of the bag and drop into hot oil. Flatten with spatula or spoon. Fry on medium hot coals and remove pan from heat every minute or two to keep from over browning or burning. It's still cooking while off the heat momentarily. When the biscuits start to firm up and are slightly browned flip to the other side and continue cooking. Again, remove from heat occasionally to keep from burning. Remove from pan and wrap in foil to stay warm until gravy is ready.

Gravy
1 pound lean ground breakfast sausage
1/3 cup all-purpose flour
½ teaspoon salt
¼ teaspoon coarse ground black pepper
3 cups milk

Crumble sausage into fry pan and cook over medium hot coals until browned and no longer pink. Stir occasionally. Wipe excess grease from pan with paper towel. Stir in flour, salt and pepper. Gradually stir in milk. Cook until mixture bubbles and thickens, stirring constantly. If gravy gets too thick add a little milk. Serve sausage mixture over warm split biscuits.

River Bites & Breaks

Stromboli Wrap
6-12 people ~ tools: can opener, spoon, tin plate

6 10 inch flour tortillas
12 thin slices deli pastrami
12 thin slices deli chicken
12 thin slices deli ham
12 thin slices deli salami
12 slices Muenster cheese
12 slices Medium Cheddar cheese
1 15 ounce bottle Pizza Squeeze sauce

Prepare one at a time on tin plate. For each tortilla layer two slices of each meat and cheese with a couple of spoons of pasta sauce. Rollup Tight. For 12 people cut in half.

Asian Chicken Wrap
4-8 people ~ tools: Slicing knife

4 10 inch flour tortillas
16 ounces deli shaved chicken breast
1 medium cucumber, chopped
4 large lettuce leaves
10 ounce jar Thai Peanut Satay sauce

For each tortilla, layer lettuce, cucumber, thai sauce and chicken. Roll tight, cut in half.

Cold Camp Tortilla Wrap
6 sandwiches ~ tools: small bowl

6 soft flour tortilla's
6 ounce container of frozen avocado dip
6 ounce container of soft cream cheese
8 ounces thin sliced sandwich turkey
8 ounces thin sliced sandwich roast beef
8 ounces sliced Monterey, pepper jack,
            muenster or other soft cheese
8 ounces sliced medium cheddar cheese
1 head leaf lettuce
8 ounce plastic bottle of mild taco sauce

Thaw avocado sauce and combine with cream cheese in a
small bowl. Mix well and spread evenly on each tortilla,
all the way to the edges. Layer meat, cheese and lettuce over
avocado sauce. Roll up. Pass the taco sauce around.

Rosebud Ham and Apple Pita
4-8 people ~ tools: Slicing knife

4 whole wheat pita bread
16 ounces thin sliced deli ham
2 large apples sliced thin
8 slices medium cheddar cheese
6 tablespoons mayonnaise or Miracle Whip
Optional: top with sliced strawberries

Slice Pita in half and spread the inside with Mayonnaise.
Divide the ham, cheese and apple among the pita halves.

Nancy's River Sandwich
6 people ~ tools knife, spoon

1 cup of cubed Cheddar Cheese
1 cup of cubed Swiss Cheese
1 cup of cauliflower broken into small pieces
2 stalks of celery diced
1 carrot grated
2 cups of cubed leftover cooked turkey, chicken or ham
6 Pita Bread
mayonnaise and/or mustard

AT Home:
Cube ham, turkey, broccoli, cauliflower,
Cheddar cheese and pepper jack cheese.
Mix and put into a seal tight plastic bag. Keep in cooler.

On the River: Spread inside of Pita Bread with mayonnaise
& mustard. Stuff with sandwich mix.
(*A fun trip with Nancy Good)*

Yellow Submarine
4 people ~ tools: Slicing knife

2 twelve inch hoagie rolls
¼ cup butter or margarine
16 ounces sliced deli ham
8 ounces sliced swiss cheese
8 ounces sliced cheddar cheese
1 cup pepperoncini
1 yellow bell pepper
½ cup creamy Italian Dressing

Slice Bread in half lengthwise. Spread softened butter over
the bottom half. Layer with ham, cheese, pepperoncini and
sliced bell pepper. Drizzle with Italian Dressing. Top with
remaining bread. Cut in two for four servings.

Veggie Pita
3-6 people ~ tools: Slicing knife

3 whole wheat pita bread, cut in half
10 ounces roasted red pepper hummus
2 tomatoes, cut into thin slices
1 cucumber, cut into thin slices
1 red onion cut into thin slices
1 green pepper, cut into thin strips

Slice Pita in half and spread the inside with hummus.
Divide remaining ingredients among the 4 pita halves

Bacon Egg Salad Sandwich
4 people~ tools: Slicing knife

2 6 inch hoagie rolls
2 tablespoons butter or margarine
4 slices Canadian bacon
Pkg of 6 prepared hard boiled eggs from refrigerator isle
2 tablespoons mayonnaise
1 tablespoon Dijon mustard or Durkees® dressing
1 beefsteak tomato
4 romaine lettuce leaves

Slice rolls in half and spread with butter. Top with lettuce.
Slice eggs onto lettuce and lightly chop. Spread with mayo
and Dijon. Top with sliced tomato and Canadian Bacon.

Afternoon Delight

Port Wine Cheese & Red Seedless Grapes

Cut cheese in wedges. Arrange on serving plate with grapes.
Crackers optional.

Roast Beef Horseradish Roll Ups

4 people ~ tools: small bowl, spoon, plate, toothpicks

1 pound sliced deli roast beef
8 ounce package soft cream cheese
2 tablespoons prepared horseradish
1 tablespoon Dijon mustard
16 ounce jar whole baby dill pickles

Combine cream cheese, horseradish and mustard in a bowl
and mix until well blended. Place one slice of roast beef on a
plate, spread with cream cheese, horseradish, mustard mix.
Place a pickle on one side of the roast beef and roll up with
the pickle in the center. Secure with toothpick.
Repeat with remaining ingredients.

Roast Beef & Blue Crostini

6-8 people ~ tools: serving plate or dish, knife

1   pound deli roast beef, shaved
10 ounce package prepared crostini
1   small jar horseradish mustard
5   ounce blue cheese wedge

Arrange Sliced Roast Beef, Sliced Blue Cheese Wedge, and
Crostini on serving plate with horseradish mustard.

Kalamata Olive Bruschetta
4 people ~ tools: sharp knife, serving plate

10 ounce jar Kalamata Olive Tapenade
8 ounce Goat Cheese Log
12 ounce package Bruschetta Rosemary and Olive Oil Toast

Spread Bruschetta with Olive Tapenade and top with a slice of goat cheese. Allow to sit a few minutes before serving to allow juice from tapenade to settle into the bruschetta.

Horseradish Asparagus Roll Ups
6-8 people ~ tools: sharp knife, high sided sheet pan, spatula

12 large stalks of asparagus
9 ounce jar cream style horseradish sauce
12 thin slices deli roast beef or pastrami (about one pound)
2 cups water
¼ cup olive oil
salt
black pepper

Cut off the tough fibrous ends of the asparagus. Place the sheet pan on the grill over hot coals. Pour water into the pan. Add the asparagus and drizzle with olive oil. Cook until water evaporates and asparagus is tender, 10 to 15 minutes. Season with salt and pepper. Remove from heat.

Spread slices of meat with horseradish and roll up one at a time with asparagus in the middle. Place back on the sheet pan and serve.

Mushroom Toasted Baguette

6-8 people ~ tools: sharp knife, high sided sheet pan, aluminum foil, spatula

1 baguette
16 ounces sliced fresh mushrooms
8 ounces muenster or swiss cheese slices
½ teaspoon Webers® Garlic and Herb Seasoning
olive oil
2 tablespoons butter

Slice baguette into ½ inch thick slices. Drizzle both sides of baguette with olive oil and place on the sheet pan, Place sheet pan on the grill over hot coals. Toast both sides. Wrap toast in aluminum foil and keep warm by the side of the grill.

Drizzle olive oil onto the sheet pan. Add butter and mushrooms. Sprinkle with garlic and herb seasoning. Sauté until mushrooms are lightly browned and toasted. Push mushrooms to the center of the pan. Arrange toast around the sides of the pan. Top mushrooms with cheese. Serve when cheese is melted.

Frans Roasted & Toasted

4 people ~ tools: aluminum foil, sharp knife, bread board, 4 wooden skewers

6 slices Texas Toast ~ *thicker sliced white bread*
¼ pound butter or margarine
12 ounces thin sliced pastrami
12 ounces thin sliced ham
12 ounces thin sliced turkey
8 ounces sliced pepper jack cheese
8 ounces sliced cheddar cheese
12 cherry tomatoes
spicy brown mustard
spray olive oil

Spray four squares of heavy duty aluminum foil with olive oil. Cut Texas Toast into quarter slices. Butter both sides of the bread. Skewer the meat, tomato and cheese between bread slices, dividing equally between the four skewers. Wrap individually in the foil and heat over medium coals for about 15 to 20 minutes, turning occasionally until bread is lightly toasted and cheese is melty.

Serve with spicy brown mustard.

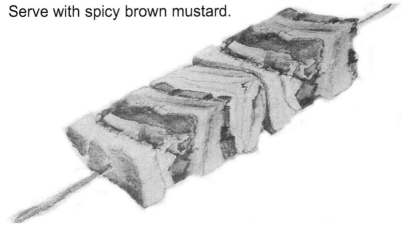

Cheddar Beer Fondue Kabobs
4 to 6 people ~ tools: can opener, 2 tin foil cake pans with high sides, stirring spoon, can opener

Fondue

4 cups shredded sharp cheddar cheese
2 tablespoons cornstarch mixed in with cheese
1 12 ounce can light beer
½ teaspoon Dijon mustard
¼ teaspoon hot sauce
Canola oil spray

Place a few pebbles in the bottom of one pan and add water to the top of the pebbles. Place the other pan on top of the pebbles. Mix beer, mustard and hot sauce into the pan and place on grill over medium hot coals. Stir in the cheese with cornstarch. Continue to stir until the cheese is melted and smooth.

Kabobs
Tools: wooden skewers, soaked in water for 10 minutes

2 pounds cooked Kielbasa sausage
1 29 ounce can whole new potatoes
1 head of broccoli
olive oil

Slice Kielbasa into 2 inch thick pieces. Cut Florets from the broccolli. Chop the remaining broccoli stalks into tiny pieces and toss into the cheese fondue. Open the potatoes and skewer the broccoli between the kielbasa and potatoes. Drizzle with olive oil. Roast on the grill turning often until everything is browned. Dip into the Cheese Fondue.

Horse Prairie Chicken

4 to 6 people ~ tools: wooden skewers, soaked in water for 10 minutes, gallon size seal tight plastic bag

5 skinless boneless chicken breast halves
1 cup ranch dressing
4 tablespoons Worcestershire Sauce
½ cup olive oil

Stir ranch dressing and Worcestershire together in a gallon size seal tight plastic bag. Cut chicken into skewer size lengths (½ inch x length of breast) and toss into dressing mix. Relax, give it 30 minutes or more in the cooler. Mix in the olive oil. Thread the chicken onto skewers, and discard dressing.

Place chicken on a lightly oiled grill over medium hot coals turning occasionally until chicken is no longer pink and juice is clear. Serve with more ranch dressing.

Asian Chicken Kabobs

4 to 6 people ~ tools: wooden skewers, soaked in water for 10 minutes, gallon size seal tight plastic bag

5 skinless boneless chicken breast halves
1 tablespoon Siracha Hot Chili Sauce
½ cup Teriyaki sauce
½ cup olive oil
Serve with sweet chili sauce or kung pao sauce

Stir seasoning together in a gallon size seal tight plastic bag. Cut chicken into two inch pieces and mix in bag with seasoning. Relax, give it 30 minutes or more in the cooler. Mix in the olive oil. Thread the chicken onto skewers, and discard dressing. Place chicken on a lightly spray oiled grill over medium hot coals. Turn occasionally until chicken is no longer pink and juice is clear.

Rivers and Rafts One Pan or No Pan Meals
Sometimes the easiest foods are the most satisfying

Marie's Wild Rice Soup
5-6 people ~ tools: 5 quart soup pot, soup ladle, soup cups

4 ounce box Long Grain and Wild Rice Mix
1 ½ cups water
1 shredded carrot ~ *easier pre shredded organic carrot*
2 cups chopped fully cooked ham
2 green onions, finely chopped
2 tablespoons butter
32 ounce carton reduced sodium chicken broth
12 ounce can evaporated milk
3 ounce package sliced almonds
salt and pepper

At Home: Grate carrot, chop ham and pack in a seal tight plastic bag.

In Camp: Sauté onions in the soup pot with butter over medium coals. Transfer onions from pan to a soup bowl. Pour water into soup pot and bring to a boil, add rice to boiling water. Lower heat to simmer the rice until tender, about 25 minutes. Pour in chicken broth and evaporated milk and heat over medium to hot coals, stir often. Add onion, ham, carrots and almonds. Simmer 5 to 10 minutes.

Serve with:
Horse Prairie Chicken or Asian Chicken Kabobs ~ page 117

Green Chili Chicken Soup
4 people ~ tools: soup pot, soup ladle, tin cups, spoons

1 10 ounce can Green Chili Enchilada sauce
1 16 ounce can reduced sodium Chicken Broth
2 pounds boneless skinless Chicken Breast
   Or rotisserie chicken, shredded
2 cups shredded Medium Cheddar cheese
1 10 ounce bag Tortilla Chips ~ *corn chips are also good*
8   ounce sour cream

At Home: Cut chicken into cubes and sauté' in olive oil.
Pack in a seal tight plastic bag, Freeze.

In Camp: Combine enchilada sauce, chicken broth and
cooked chicken in soup pot. Heat on grill over low flame
or hot coals, stir often.

To Serve: Ladle soup into cups, top with shredded
cheese and sour cream. Dip up your soup with tortilla
chips.

Tostada's Salad
4 people ~ tools: aluminum foil, knife

4 pre-baked Tortilla Salad Bowls
1 15 ounce can Black Beans
2 heads Icebergs Lettuce or prepackaged shredded lettuce
12 ounces shredded Mexican Cheese blend
12 ounce jar Chipotle Ranch Dressing
6   ounce can Sliced Black Olives

Chop lettuce and divide into tortilla bowls. Open beans and
drain liquid. Pour ½ cup water into beans and shake to rinse
the beans. Drain water. Spoon beans over lettuce. Top with
cheese, dressing and olives.

Quick Ravioli Soup
6 people ~ tools: 5 quart soup pot, serving spoon, soup bowls or cups

15 ounce can pizza sauce
2 ~ 12 ounce bottles low sodium V8 vegetable juice
15 ounce can low sodium beef broth
16 ounce bag frozen mini meatballs
20 ounce bag four cheese mini ravioli
1 tablespoon olive oil
1 bag seasoned garlic croutons
2 cups freshly grated parmesan cheese

Thaw meatballs and ravioli. Combine beef broth, pizza sauce and V8 in soup pot. Heat over hot coals. Move pot to the side of the grill and add meatballs and ravioli. Simmer about 10 minutes until meatballs are hot. Ladle into serving bowls or cups and sprinkle with croutons and parmesan.

Buttermilk Biscuits
4 people ~ tools: 2 round aluminum foil cake pans

1 can refrigerated Buttermilk Biscuits
Crisco vegetable shortening

Grease 1 of the cake pans and arrange the biscuits in the pan. Cover and set in a warm spot for 20 minutes or until biscuits have doubled in size. Place a few small pebbles in the other pan and pour in enough water to just cover the pebbles. Place the pan with the biscuits on top of the pebbles and cook over hot coals for about 20 minutes.

New England Clam Chowder and Biscuits

4 people ~ tools: large saucepan, 2 round foil cake pans
large serving spoon, sharp knife

4 slices bacon
2 potatoes, peeled and diced
1 stalk celery, finely chopped
2 green onions, chopped
2 6 ounce cans minced clams, save the liquid
4 cups water
2 tablespoons butter or margarine
1 cup dry powdered whole milk
½ cup dehydrated mashed potatoes
salt and pepper

1 can refrigerated Buttermilk Biscuit Dough
Reserved bacon grease.

Peel and cut the potatoes into small pieces. Chop the celery
and onions. Cut each slice of bacon in half.
In large saucepan cook bacon until it is crispy. Remove
bacon to a plate or bowl and crumble before everyone eats it.
Keep the bacon grease.

Hide the Bacon! Prepare the Biscuits.
Grease 1 of the cake pans and arrange the biscuits in the
pan. Cover and set in a warm spot for 20 minutes or until
biscuits have doubled in size. Place a few small pebbles in
the other cake pan and pour in enough water to just cover
the pebbles. Place the pan with the biscuits on top of the
pebbles and cook over hot coals for about 20 minutes.

Saute the potatoes, celery and onion in the bacon grease.
Open the clams and drain the liquid into the pan. Pour water
into the pan then slowly stir in the powdered milk until it
dissolves. Stir in the dehydrated mashed potatoes. Add
butter, salt and pepper. Garnish each serving with bacon.

French Bread Pizza
6-8 people ~ tools: heavy duty aluminum foil, sharp knife

Traditional

One loaf of Garlic Buttered French Bread
  cut in half lengthwise

1 16 ounce can Italian spaghetti sauce
1 16 slice package mozzarella cheese
1 8 ounce package pepperoni slices
1 4 ounce can sliced black olives
cooking oil

Brush the outside of the bread with olive oil and place each half of the bread on separate lengths of aluminum foil. Spread each half with spaghetti sauce all the way to the edges. Top with cheese, pepperoni and olives. Place on the grill over medium low coals. Cover lightly with foil and bake until cheese is warm and runny.

Garlic Chicken Pizza

One loaf of Garlic Buttered French Bread
  cut in half lengthwise
1 16 ounce can alfredo sauce
1 16 slice package mozzarella cheese
8 ounce pre-package rotisserie chicken pieces
2 bell peppers *red and green* cleaned and chopped
cooking oil.

Follow directions above for Traditional pizza.

Steak and Shrimp Skewers with Roasted Asparagus

4 people ~ tools: 8 wooden skewers soaked in water to keep from burning, grill, heavy aluminum foil, cooks leather glove

1 pound asparagus
2 Tenderloin Steaks
1 pound bag of fantail shrimp
2 bell peppers (yellow and orange) cut into large squares
12 cherry tomatoes
olive oil
lemon juice
salt, black pepper
gorgonzola Cheese

Trim asparagus and lay out on a 16 inch sheet of heavy aluminum foil. Drizzle with olive oil. Sprinkle with salt and pepper. Wrap in foil, creating a flat package. Place over medium coals to bake for 10 to 15 minutes turning occasionally. Sprinkle with gorgonzola cheese before serving.

Sprinkle lemon juice on shrimp and allow to set. Cut steak into thin strips. Cut peppers into large squares. Layer steak peppers, shrimp and tomatoes on skewer. Brush with olive oil. And place on grill over medium coals turning often until done.

Peggy's Pesto Pasta and Garlic Toast

6-8 people ~ tools: high sided fry pan
serving spoon, aluminum foil, can opener

Pasta

12 ounces Thin Spaghetti noodles
4 cups water
4 tablespoons olive oil
1 18 inch length of aluminum foil

Bring water to a boil over medium hot coals. Add 1 tablespoon olive oil and thin spaghetti, Water should just cover the spaghetti. Boil 8 to 10 minutes or until noodles are tender. Drain any excess water and drizzle with additional olive oil. Make a boat of your aluminum foil and pour noodles into the foil. Wrap into a package and seal. Place to the side of your grill to keep warm. Prepare Pesto

Pesto

1/2 cup olive oil
1 onion diced
8 ounce package sliced mushrooms
3 ounce package sun dried tomatoes, julienne cut
3/4 cup dry red wine
1 ounce package garlic and herb dip seasoning mix
1 4 ounce can chopped black olives
1 cup grated parmesan cheese

Place fry pan on grill over medium hot coals. Pour in olive oil. When the oil is hot add onions and mushrooms. Stir for a few minutes until onion turns translucent Add wine and sun dried tomatoes, stir in seasoning mix. Allow to simmer until the tomatoes soften and wine is reduced. Gently fold the pasta into the sauce. Top with cheese and olives.

Garlic Bread ~ packaged in aluminum foil, toasted on grill

Erica's Creole Rice

4 people ~ tools: 1 large cook pot, spoon,
tin plate for pot lid

1 pound fully cooked polish sausage

1 pound pre-cooked Extra Large or Jumbo frozen shrimp

2 cups minute rice or Rice a Roni® Chicken and Vegetables

1 pkg. Cajun Sauce seasoning mix

2 six ounce cans low sodium V8® Vegetable Juice

2 cups water

Thaw shrimp and drain any liquid, set aside.
Slice the sausage into large bite size pieces and put into the cook pot over hot coals to brown. Add shrimp. Pour in the water and V8 juice. Stir in seasoning mix. Bring to a boil over small flame or hot coals. Adjust temperature so the sauce just simmers. Add minute rice, stir once. Cover and remove from heat. Allow to set for five minutes or until rice is cooked.

Note: The V8 cans provide extra water and are easy to crush and pack out in the seal tight bag you brought for garbage.

Pork Chops and Beans

4 people ~ tools: large fry pan, heavy aluminum foil,
Large serving spoon

4-6 lean boneless pork chops
3 15ounce cans of Pork and Beans
Heavy Aluminum Foil
¼ cup Canola Oil

Line fry pan with foil. Pour in Canola oil to heat over hot coals. Sear Pork Chops in the hot oil, turning once. Move the pan to medium coals. Stack the pork chops on one side of the pan and add beans to the pan. Heat until very hot. Serve on tin plates.

Quick Stir Fry

4 people ~ tools: high side fry pan, heavy aluminum foil,
large serving spoon

1 pound beef sirloin, sliced thinly
2 cups fresh broccoli florets
1 red bell pepper, sliced discard seed and stem
2 carrots, julienned
1 green onion, chopped
1 teaspoon minced garlic
2 teaspoons soy sauce
2 teaspoons toasted sesame seeds
2 tablespoons canola oil

Heat oil in fry pan on grill over hot coals. Add sliced beef and fry 3-4 minutes. Add vegetables and stir fry until carrots are soft. Season with soy sauce and sesame seeds.

Trout with Herbs and Feta Cheese

4 people ~ tools: large fry pan, spatula

2 large trout Fillets
Lemon Pepper Herb Seasoning (we like Webers Grill)
2 Roma tomatoes, thick sliced
4 one to two inch sprigs fresh basil
4 one to two inch sprigs fresh oregano
¼ cup crumbled Feta Cheese
¼ cup canola oil

Heat oil in fry pan over hot coals. Season fish fillets with
Lemon Pepper and place in fry pan. Brown on both sides,
flipping only once. Move pan to medium coals. Arrange the
tomato slices around the sides of the fish. Sprinkle with basil
and oregano. Allow to cook until flaky. Sprinkle with
crumbled Feta cheese immediately before serving.

Smith River ~ a big catch

127

How to Filet a Fish

Let your fish air dry for a few minutes so it won't be as slippery. Lay fish on a newspaper (or a filet board) Insert a filet knife under the gill and atop the bone. Slice down to the tail. Do not cut off the tail but flip the fish over and repeat on the other side. Discard the fish head and bones. Flip the meat over so the skin is on the newspaper and holding onto the tail, slice between the skin and the filet. Do not wet the filet. If it gets dirty wipe it off with a paper towel.

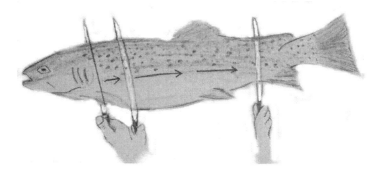

For more information check online in: "The Art of Manliness. How To Fillet a Fish" ~ A very interesting website with lots of information for the ladies also.

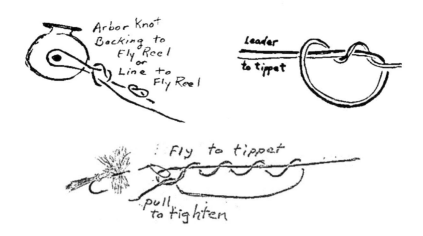

Charlie's Fried Trout with Hash Browns and Onions
6 people: Tools / grill, fry pan, aluminum foil, spatula

2-3 Fresh Caught Trout depending on size
½ cup cornmeal
½ cup flour
salt and pepper
canola oil
one sliced onion
1 28 ounce bag frozen Hash Browns

Clean trout and cut the head and tail off. Salt and pepper the inside of the fish. Heat fry pan over hot coals. Pour enough oil in the pan to lightly coat the bottom. Toss in the hash browns and allow to crisp. Flip and crisp the other side. Salt and pepper the potatoes and wrap in a sheet of aluminum foil. Set potatoes to the side to keep warm.

Mix corn meal, flour, salt and pepper in a large zip lock bag. Drop fish into the bag and shake to coat with flour mix. Add a bit more canola oil to the fry pan and heat again over hot coals. Place the fish in the pan and cook until the center of the fish flakes with a fork.

Add the sliced onion to the pan. Flip your fish and cook the other side. About 5 to 7 minutes per side. Serve hot with potatoes.

Tip: Save leftover fish in a small zip lock bag. Mix with mustard, onion and pickles. Serve on crackers for lunch the next day.

Photo and fish belong to Ben Racicot

129

Steak on a Stick

6 people ~ tools: 6 clean and sharpened green willow branches, sharp knife, cutting board

6 Bacon Wrapped Tenderloin Steaks or Top Sirloin
1 bottle Worcestershire Sauce
1 pound bacon
spray canola oil
Webers® Steak & Chop seasoning
meat tenderizer
steak sauce

Slice Top Sirloin Steaks into two inch wide strips. Lightly sprinkle steaks with meat tenderizer.   Drizzle with Worcestershire and lightly sprinkle on seasoning. Thread steak strips onto green willow sticks. Spray with Canola oil and roast over hot campfire coals (NOT FLAMES)

Optional Bacon: wrap bacon strips around steak and secure with toothpicks.

 Serve with New potatoes and fresh mushrooms page 131

New Potatoes and Button Mushrooms

6 people ~ tools: aluminum foil lasagna pan, aluminum foil, Serving spoon, can opener

12 small new potatoes
    Or 3 15 ounce cans Whole New Potatoes
8 ounce container of fresh button mushrooms
2 tablespoon olive oil
2 tablespoons fresh butter
Salt and Pepper
1 cup of water

Quarter potatoes and place in a foil pan with 1 cup of water, Place the foil pan on grill over hot coals, cover with foil. Add water if necessary until water steam cooks the potatoes. (*or open canned new potatoes and drain water*)

Drizzle olive oil into the pan and warm enough for the oil to spread around the bottom of the pan. When the potatoes are soft push them to the outsides of the pan. Drizzle a little more oil in the bottom of the pan. Put the fresh mushrooms in the center of the pan along with the butter. Salt and Pepper everything. Cook until the mushroom juice runs like a gravy. Stir gently as needed.

Don't sleep with your boots on!

Some years ago I found myself being kicked in front of the campfire. It was a friendly, hey wake up, kind of kick so I woke up. "Get up we are going to bed" I was told, so I tried to get up. I could not move my feet to get up!

My kind husband and brother Andy reached out and pulled me to my feet. I could not walk! They laughed at me.

"Come on" I was told. "Seriously," I replied, "My feet won't move!" The final investigation revealed that I had slept with my feet too close to the fire and my boots had melted together. Dang! I really should have kept those boots to prove my story is true. I do have witness's, however.

131

Cajun New York Steak

*4 people ~ tools: large griddle or cast iron steak plates,
tin plates, spatula*

4 New York Strip Steaks
1/2 cup Worcestershire Sauce
2 Tablespoons Tabasco®
1 tablespoon brown sugar
1 tablespoon red wine vinegar
2 Tablespoons Webers® N'Orleans Cajun Seasoning

Olive oil
Coarse Ground Black Pepper
steak sauce

At Home: Combine Worcestershire, Tabasco, Sugar,
Vinegar & Cajun seasoning in a gallon size seal tight plastic
freezer bag. Mix well. Add steaks and seal tight. Freeze.

*Steaks should thaw and marinate for a night and a day in the
cooler. Once thawed, flip a few times to distribute the
seasoning.*

In Camp: Remove steaks from the marinade. Drizzle with
olive oil, sprinkle with **coarse** ground black pepper. Place
griddle on the grill over hot coals. When griddle is hot enough
for a drop of water to sizzle, put steaks on the grill and cook
about 8 minutes per side or to your liking. Do not cut into the
meat to check if it is cooked enough.   Remove from heat and
let rest for 5 to 10 minutes to gather the juices back into the
meat. If someone wants their steak more done, they can put
it back on the grill.

*Serve with New Potatoes and Mushrooms pg. 131
Or 2 10 ounce packages Birds Eye Frozen Potato Vegetable Blend*

Sweet and Spicy Chicken Kabobs with Quinoa
6 people ~ tools: wooden skewers

3 large boneless, skinless chicken breasts
1 large yellow squash
1 large zucchini
2 red bell peppers
6 medium size fresh mushrooms

Sweet and Spicy Glaze
¾ cup honey
½ cup hot and spicy mustard
2 tablespoons soy sauce.

Soak wooden skewers in water for 15 minutes. Cut chicken and vegetables into bite size pieces. Thread onto skewers and brush with honey mustard. Place grill 6 inches above hot coals. Grill kabobs over hot coals 8 to 10 minutes, turning often. Brush with glaze again and cook another 5 minutes. Serves well with Quinoa or Rice

Quinoa *a plant based complete protein*
6 people ~ tools: medium size saucepan, serving spoon

1 ½ cups Quinoa, rinse before cooking to remove bitter taste
3 cups water
1 tablespoon butter, sprinkle of salt and/or lemon pepper

Pour water and butter into the saucepan and bring to a boil over hot coals. Add Quinoa and reduce heat to medium coals. Allow to simmer *not boil* for 15 minutes. Cover with foil and let the quinoa steam for 5 minutes longer. Fluff with fork. *(Try quinoa at home to be sure you like it. If not, substitute rice for quinoa.*

Minute Steak with Roasted Potatoes and Vegetables
4 people ~ tools: grill, fry pan, tin plate, spatula

4 large thick cube steaks, *meat tenderizer optional*
½ can beer
1 teaspoon Worcestershire®
4 large potatoes, cleaned and cut into bite size chunks
4 carrots cleaned and sliced into 1 inch pieces
1 envelope Lipton onion soup mix
 ⅓ cup canola oil
salt and pepper
optional: sour cream, steak sauce

Heat the pan over hot coals, coat the bottom of the pan with oil. Sear steaks on both sides. Sprinkle on salt, pepper and Worcestershire. Add beer and reduce heat to simmer. Move steaks to tin a plate and set to the side of grill to keep warm and to continue slow cooking.

Cut potatoes and slice carrots. Pour remaining oil into the fry pan and return to hot coals. Add carrots and potatoes, stirring to brown on all sides. Stir in onion soup mix and juice from the steak. Put steak on top of the potatoes. Cover the steak with a tin plate while allowing steam to escape from the vegetables. Reduce heat and continue cooking until vegetables are tender, about 20 minutes.

Hobbit Steak
4 people ~ tools: 1 frypan, spatula, sharp knife

2 pounds top sirloin steak, tenderized.
1 large Kielbasa sausage about 16 ounces
2 green peppers cut into bite size squares
1 red onion cut into bite size squares and separated
8 oz. fresh mushrooms
3 Tablespoons Worchestershire® Sauce
1 teaspoon coarse ground black pepper
4 slices of thin sliced bacon

Cook bacon until crispy over medium hot coals. Enjoy the bacon. One slice each. Saute the onion in the bacon grease. Yes, It is essential to the flavor. Add remaining ingredients and cook until steak is done. Serve over mashed potatoes or cooked rice.

Mashed Potatoes
4 people ~ 8x8 alluminum foil pan, serving spoon

2 four ounce packages Idaho Mashed Potatoes
3 tablespoons butter
4 cups water

Pour water into foil pan and bring to a boil over hot coals. Move to the side of the grill. Open potatoes and pour all at once into the boiling water. Stirring at the same time.
Top with butter. Divide potatoes equally among plates and Spoon Hobbit Steak over the potatoes.

Rice

2 cups rice
3 cups water
3 tablespoons butter

Same directions as mashed potatoes except ~ after pouring rice into the boiling water reduce heat and allow to simmer for 20 to 30 minutes. Do not stir more than once.

Beef Stroganoff

4-6 people ~ tools: 1 large cook pot with lid,
8x12 alluminum foil cake pan, can opener, sharp knife,
serving spoon

2 pounds cube steak cut into strips
2 tablespoons canola oil
1 onion chopped
2 cups fresh sliced mushrooms
1 teaspoon minced garlic
1 can cream of mushroom soup
1 teaspoon Worcestershire sauce
1 cup of sour cream
1 12 ounce package wide egg noodles
4 cups water

Pour water into the cook pot and bring to a boil over hot coals. Add a tablespoon of oil to the water to keep the noodles from sticking. Add the noodles and cook until noodles are tender, about 10 minutes. Drain water from the noodles and drizzle with oil to keep noodles from sticking. Stir once and pour into foil pan.   Set to the side of the grill to keep warm.

Wipe cook pot with a paper towel. Pour oil into cook pot and place on the grill over hot coals. Toss in steak strips to sizzle and brown. Add onions mushrooms and garlic to brown with the steak, then add mushroom soup and Worcestershire. Stir and set to the side of the grill to simmer.

Pour sour cream over noodles and stir. Serve steak over noodles.

Salisbury Steak

4 people ~ tools: 1 large fry pan, spatula, can opener,
2 tin plates, serving spoon, zip lock bag

1½ pounds ground beef
1 egg
6 crushed saltine crackers
2 tablespoons dried chopped onion
¼ teaspoon poultry seasoning mix
½ teaspoon salt
½ teaspoon pepper
12 ounces fresh sliced mushrooms
3 tablespoons butter
1 package brown gravy mix
1½ cups water

Serve with Toast or Hash Browns

AT HOME: Mix together ground beef, egg, cracker crumbs, onion, salt, poultry seasoning with your hands and pack into a quart size seal tight plastic bag and freeze.

IN CAMP, prepare cook fire. Heat pan with oil over medium hot coals. Shape the ground beef mixture into 4 patties and fry on both sides until done. Stack on a tin plate at the side of the grill and cover with another plate to keep warm.

Wipe out any grease with a paper towel. Lightly saute' mushrooms in the pan with butter. Add water and stir in gravy mix. Return the beef to the gravy pan and simmer over low coals until gravy thickens. Just a few minutes. Remove from heat so gravy doesn't overcook.

Chicken and Dumplings
4 people ~ tools: 1 large cook pot with lid, big serving spoon

4 boneless skinless chicken breasts
¼ cup canola oil
1 2 ounce packet creamy chicken alfredo seasoning mix
1 12 ounce can evaporated milk
1 14 ounce can chicken broth
1 cup water

Heat oil in the cook pot over medium coals. Cut the chicken into bite size pieces and drop into the hot oil. Stir to brown on all sides. Add water and stir in seasoning mix. Add milk and chicken broth. Set to the side and prepare dumplings.

Dumplings

1 cup flour
2 ½ teaspoons baking powder
½ teaspoon salt
½ cup milk
1 egg
margarine
quart size zip lock bag

Coat the zip lock bag with margarine. Mix the baking powder and salt with the flour and put into zip lock with the milk and egg. Seal and squish together until dough is formed. Drop by spoonful's into bubbling chicken and noodles. Cover pot tightly and cook over medium coals for about 15 minutes. Keep the liquid boiling gently and do not uncover the pot during cooking.

Easier ~ you can make dumplings with bisquick but the dumplings will be drier.

Chicken and Broccoli Stir Fry

4 people ~ tools: large high sided fry pan, spatula or spoon

3 boneless skinless chicken breasts
2 tablespoons canola oil
1 teaspoon toasted sesame oil
4 Sliced green onions
1 bunch of broccoli
11 ounce jar Stir Fry Sauce of your choosing
Peanuts Optional

At Home:
Cut Chicken Breasts into bite size pieces and freeze in a seal tight plastic freezer bag. Cut broccoli into small florets. Discard the tough stem and pack in seal tight bag.

In Camp:
Drain all liquid from the chicken and pat dry with a paper towel. Heat 2 tablespoons canola oil in high sided fry pan. Add chicken and brown over hot coals. Season with Salt and Pepper. Cook for about 5 minutes stirring occasionally until chicken is browned and mostly cooked through. Add sesame oil, green onion, and broccoli to the chicken and stir to combine. Reduce heat and cook until broccoli is bright green. Pour in Stir Fry Sauce and heat until bubbly.

Serve with Jasmine Rice

4 people ~ tools: saucepan with lid or foil

2 cups rice
2 cups water
2 tablespoons butter

Pour water into sauce pan and place on grill over hot coals. When water boils, stir in rice and butter. Cover with lid or foil. Move to the side of the grill and continue to cook for about 20 minutes or until water is absorbed. Fluff with a fork.

Sloppy Joes
4 people ~ tools: 1 large cook pot with lid, big serving spoon

2 tablespoons canola oil
2 ½ pounds lean ground beef
salt and pepper
1 onion, chopped
1 green pepper chopped
1 cup tomato ketchup
1 cup barbeque sauce
½ cup water
2 tablespoons brown sugar
4 large hamburger buns or hoagie rolls

Heat oil in cook pot over hot coals. Add ground beef to the pan in small pieces and stir until browned. Pour off any excess oil or water. Season with salt and pepper. Add onion and green pepper. Sauté over medium coals for 5 minutes. Add water and stir in brown sugar, ketchup and barbeque sauce. Move pot to the side of the grill to simmer. Enjoy a beer, you earned it. Serve on buns or hoagie rolls.

Upside Down Taco's
4 people ~ tools: 1 large cook pot with lid, big serving spoon

2 pounds lean ground beef
1 ounce package taco seasoning
1 15 ounce can chili with beans
1 12 ounce package shredded cheddar cheese
1 12 ounce bag Frito's Corn Chips Scoops

Cook ground beef in cook pot or skillet on the grill over hot coals, stir occasionally until no longer pink. Remove from heat. Wipe grease out of the pan with a paper towel and burn the paper. Open chili and add to the ground beef. Return to coals, stirring occasionally until bubbly hot. Spoon over corn chips, top with cheese.

Crazy Mountain Hash
4 people ~ tools: large fry pan, spatula

2 pounds ground beef
2 medium onions, chopped
1 large green pepper, chopped
1 8 ounce can kidney beans
1 8 ounce can golden hominy, liquid drained
½ teaspoon Italian seasoning
salt and pepper
Garlic Bread
Tabasco sauce

Cook crumbled ground beef in a large fry pan over medium hot coals. Drain any water and grease. Stir in onions, green pepper and seasoning. Sauté together for a few minutes. Add hominy and kidney beans, simmer uncovered, stirring occasionally until flavors are blended.

Serve with Garlic Bread and Tabasco sauce

French Dip Melt
4 people ~ tools: large fry pan, spatula

1 ½ pounds very thin slices of deli roast beef
4 sliced deli provolone cheese
1 can condensed French onion soup
4 hoagie rolls

Heat roast beef and onion soup together in the frypan over hot coals until liquid boils. Remove from heat. Top with cheese and pile onto hoagie rolls.

Fettuccine Alfredo

4 people ~ tools: high sided fry pan, serving spoon, slicing knife, aluminum foil

2 boneless skinless chicken breasts
2 tablespoons canola oil
Salt and pepper

1 ½ cups whole milk
1 12 ounce can chicken broth
1 tsp chopped garlic or garlic seasoning
8 ounce package fettuccini noodles

½ cup heavy cream
1 cup freshly grated parmesan

Warm oil in frypan over hot coals and add chicken. Season with salt and pepper. Cook until chicken is lightly browned and no longer pink, turning once. Slice chicken in the pan then remove chicken from the pan onto a square of aluminum foil. Wrap lightly and set by the side of the grill to keep warm.

Add chicken broth, milk, and garlic to the pan and heat over medium hot coals until the liquid simmers. Add fettuccini and cook 8 to 10 minutes stirring occasionally.

Add cream and parmesan and stir until combined. Season again with salt and pepper. Remove from heat and stir in sliced chicken. Serve immediately.

To make clean up easier, pour water and dish soap into the pan and return to the grill to simmer.

Fried Ravioli and Chicken
4 to 6 people ~ tools: 1 large high side fry pan, spatula, can opener, 16 inch sheet aluminum foil

4 boneless skinless chicken breasts, cut in half
½ cup canola oil
Salt and pepper
1 red onion
3 Roma tomatoes
Garlic pepper seasoning
24 ounce package large ravioli ~ beef or cheese
8 ounces crumbled feta cheese
slivered almonds

Pour about 2 tablespoons oil in frypan. Place on the grill over hot coals and add chicken. Salt and pepper the chicken. Turn when browned on one side and cooked halfway through.

Cut onion into thin slices and cut slices in half. Sauté with the chicken. When chicken is done, wrap it with the onion in foil and move to the side of the grill to keep warm.

Heat the remaining oil in the fry pan. Add ravioli to the hot oil, reduce heat and allow ravioli to fry on one side. Sprinkle lightly with garlic seasoning. Gently flip ravioli with spatula, trying not to break them up.

Cut tomatoes into small pieces and add to the ravioli. Top with crumbled gorgonzola and almonds. Serve with chicken.

Double Steak Sandwich
4 people ~ tools: cutting board, sharp knife, fork,
aluminum foil

8 cube steaks
4 Kaiser Rolls
8 swiss cheese slices
1 onion
1 tomato
  soft butter or margarine
  steak & chop seasoning
  steak sauce

Slice Kaiser roll and butter each side. Wrap in aluminum foil
and set on the side of the grill to warm and soften the rolls.
Peel onion and cut into thin slices. Slice tomato.

Place steaks on the cutting board and using a washed and
dried river rock pound it lightly until very thin to make it more
tender. Sprinkle with seasoning. Place on grill over hot
coals. Cook about 4 minutes per side.

Assemble the sandwich, placing cheese onion and tomato
between two steaks on each roll.

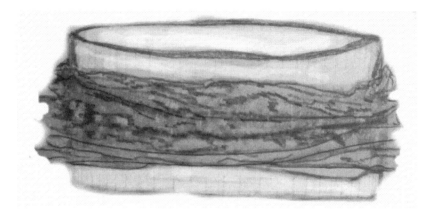

Chicken Marsall over Rice

4 people ~ tools: 1 large frypan, 1 medium size cookpot, serving spoon and sharp knife

4 boneless skinless chicken breasts, cut into bite size pieces
1 tablespoon canola oil
1 teaspoon Italian seasoning
1 teaspoon garlic powder
1 cup water
1 package spaghetti sauce mix
2 tablespoons dry brown gravy mix
¼ cup red wine
4 cups minute white rice
3 cups water

Heat oil in the frypan over hot coals. Add chicken and sauté until browned on all sides, about 5 minutes. Sprinkle on Italian seasoning and garlic and sauté for another 10 minutes until chicken juice is clear. Move chicken to the side of the pan. Pour in water and stir in spaghetti and gravy mix. Add wine.   Slide chicken into the sauce. Move pan to the side of grill so liquid simmers.

Pour water into the cookpot and bring to a boil over hot coals. Add rice to the boiling water stir once. Cover and set to the side of the grill about 30 minutes. Serve chicken over rice.

Your Just Desserts

Honey Nut Pears
4 people ~ tools: 1 8x8 inch aluminum foil pan with foil lid
spoon, small sharp knife

½ cup old fashioned rolled oats
½ cup chopped walnuts or pecans
2 tablespoons flour
        (even pancake mix works if that's what you have)
½ teaspoon cinnamon
Sprinkle of salt
2 tablespoons butter
2 tablespoons honey
2 tablespoons olive oil

2 firm semi-ripe pears
2/3 cup vanilla yogurt

Mix the oats, walnuts, flour, cinnamon and salt in the foil pan. Stir in olive oil. Place on grill over medium hot coals to brown. Stir continuously, don't burn. Remove from heat. Dot with butter and honey. Return to heat to melt in the butter and honey, mix it up. Remove from heat and push the crumbles to the side of the pan.

Cut pears in half, remove core of the pear and place in the pan. Fill each pear half with crumbles, leaving any extra to the side of the pan.

Drizzle honey over the top of each pear half. Lift the foil pan and make a little dent in the bottom with a spoon and add a wee bit of water to help the pears steam for about 15 minutes. Cover and return to the grill over medium coals. Stir a teaspoon of honey into the yogurt. Use as a topping over cooked pears.

Blueberry Cobbler

4 people ~ tools: 1 8x8 inch aluminum foil pan, 12 inch square of aluminum foil, can opener, serving spoon

1 21 ounce can Blueberry Pie Filling
1 6 ounce package blueberry muffin mix (*just add water*)
1 cup whole rolled oats
2 Tablespoon brown sugar
1 Tablespoon butter
½ cup water
Spray oil

Line the bottom of the foil pan with the square of aluminum foil. Mix the rolled oats and brown sugar and butter on the foil in the pan. Place on the grill over hot coals and stir until oatmeal starts to brown.

Remove from heat and stir in muffin mix and ½ cup water. Return to the grill and cook over low coals until the crumble starts to set up, being careful not to burn it.

With both hands carefully pull the foil with the muffin mix out of the pan and set aside. Pour Blueberry Pie filling into the foil pan and spoon the muffin mix on top of the pie filling. Cover lightly with the foil and return to the grill until the pie filling bubbles and the cobbler is cooked through.

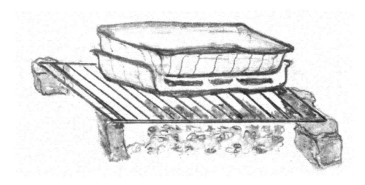

Happy Apple Nut Quesadilla's

4 people ~ tools: 4 squares non stick aluminum foil

1 15 ounce can Apple Pie Filling
6 tablespoons extra crunchy peanut butter
2 cups mini marshmallows
4 large flour tortillas
Butter Flavored Spray oil

Spray oil on one side of each tortilla and place oiled side down on open foil. Then spread the other side with peanut butter all the way to the edges. Spoon apple pie filling on top of the peanut butter dividing equally between the tortillas spread not quite to the edges. Cover with marshmallows and fold in half. Place on grill over medium coals. Turn once when tortilla is crispy. Toast the other side, serve warm.

Peaches and Cream Quesadilla's

Same as above: substitute peach pie filling for apple pie filling, omit peanut butter.

Banana Nut Croissants

4 people ~ tools: 4 squares aluminum foil

4 large croissants
4 bananas
13 ounce jar Nutella® hazelnut spread
Butter flavored spray oil

Slice croissants in half and spread Nutella generously on the inside. Slice one banana per croissant and arrange evenly inside. Spray butter flavored oil on foil and wrap one croissant on each piece of foil. Heat over medium low coals about 5 minutes per side.

Huckleberry Pie

4 people ~ tools: 1 8x8 aluminum foil baking pan, 1 square of aluminum foil, spatula or serving spoon.

1 ½ cups whole rolled oats
¼ cup butter
½ cup brown sugar
1 10 ounce jar Wild Montana Huckleberry Pie Filling
2 cups fresh huckleberries, substitute blueberries if you must

Pour rolled oats into the foil pan and place on grill over medium hot coals. Stir often until lightly toasted. Remove from heat. Mix in brown sugar. Add slices of butter and return to the grill for just a minute until butter melts. Remove from heat again and mix well, then press tightly into the bottom of the pan with a spoon. Top with the pie filling and fresh berries if you have them. Place one or two thin rocks on the grill over medium hot coals and place the pie on the rocks. Cover with foil and heat until pie filling bubbles.

Cherry Cheesecake

6-8 people ~ tools: serving spoon, paper bowls or plates

16 ounce tub refrigerated Philladelphia® cheesecake filling
1 prepared graham cracker pie crust in foil pan
1 20 ounce can cherry pie filling

Spread the cheesecake filling onto the pie crust. Top with cherry pie filling or any other fruit you like.

Big Horn Rice Pudding

8-12 people ~ tools: 2 quart cook pot

4 cups minute rice
1 cup powdered coffee creamer
2 cups raisins
6 ounce package shredded coconut
6 ounce package chopped walnuts or pecans
6 ounce package dried banana chips
6 cups water

At Home: Pour all ingredients except water and butter into a seal tight plastic bag.

In Camp: Bring water to a boil in cook pot on the grill over small flame or hot coals. Move pot to side of the grill and pour in rice mix. Stir once and allow to set for 5 to 10 minutes until rice is tender. Serve in cups or paper bowls.

Irish Coffee

tools: leather cook gloves, enameled tin coffee cup

4 ounces Hot black coffee
2 ounces Irish whiskey
1 ounce heavy whipping cream
1 teaspoon brown sugar

Pour whiskey into your tin cup and preheat next to the campfire coals for just a minute. Fill with hot coffee and stir in the sugar. Pour cream over an inverted spoon so the cream will float on top of the coffee.

BACKROADS AND CAMPERS

South Boulder River

Roads to Happiness

Libby, Kootenai Falls Swinging Bridge, Yaak River ~ Junction US hwy 2 and 508 to Yaak Falls, town of Yaak, Hwy 567 to Lake Koocanusa, 🚴🏕️🚐⛵
North Fork of the Flathead River Rd ~ West Glacier to Polebridge and Canadian Border 🏃🏕️🚴
Kallispell west on Hwy 2 to Thompson River Road hwy 556, South to Thompson Falls, North on Hwy 472, 200,56 Ross Creek Cedar Grove, Troy 🚴🏕️🚐⛵ 🏃
Rock Creek Exit 126 to Phillipsburg, Skalkaho Pass to Grantsdale, South on hwy 93 to Chief Joseph Pass, East on 43 to Wisdom, NE to 569 Mount Haggin Scenic Drive, Fairmont Hot Springs, Georgetown, Phillipsburg 🚴🏕️🚐⛵ 🏃
Black Foot River System Hwy 200 Lincoln to Bonner 🚴🏕️🚐⛵
Little Black Foot River Elliston Hwy 12W to Garrison 🚴
Pioneer Mtns ~ Wise River, Crystal Park, Polaris 🚴🏕️🏃
Big Hole River Valley ~ Dewey, Wise River, Wisdom, Jackson Hot Springs, Bannack, Dillon 🚴🏕️🚐 🏃
Dillon, Glen, Notch Bottom, Twin Bridges, Silver Star 🚴🏕️🚐
Silver Star, Virginia City, Ennis, Norris Hot Springs, Pony, South Boulder River Road 🚜 to Mammoth, Cardwell 🚴🏕️🚐
Butte, Pipestone Pass, Whitehall H-399 to Boulder Hot Springs 🚴🏕️

East Glacier Park to Augusta Hwy287, Rocky Mountain Front, Choteau, Gibson Resevoir Sun River, Augusta, Hwy 434 & 435 Bean Lake, Wolf Creek 🦕 👁 🏃 🎣 ⛰
Fort Benton Hwy 228, Shonkin, Highwood, Belt Hwy 89, Neihart, White Sulpher Springs, Smith River Road & Fort Logan, Ulm 👁 🏃 🎣 ⛰ 🛶
Helena exit 200 to Hauser Lake, York, East Shore Canyon Ferry to Townsend 🚤 👁 🏃 🎣 ⛰
Townsend on Hwy 12 & 89 & 294 to Lennep, Martinsdale Bair Museum, H-294 Ringling, Sheilds River Crazy Mountains, Clyde Park, Livingston 🚤 👁 🏃 🎣 ⛰
Big Timber, Boulder River Hwy 298 & 295 to Livingston 👁 🏃 🎣 ⛰
Yellowstone River Corridor ~ Livingston Hwy 540 south to Prey, Chico Hot Springs, Gardiner 👁 🎣
Mammoth Hot Springs, Hwy 212 to Cook City, Beartooth Highway, Red Lodge 👁 🏃 🎣 ⛰
Red Lodge Hwy 78 to Roscoe, 419 to Fishtail, Nye, Hwy 420 to Absarokee 👁 🏃 🎣 ⛰
West Yellowstone, over Targhee Pass to Henry's Lake Idaho, Red Rock Lakes National Wildlife Refuge, Centennial Valley, Monida 🎣 ⛰ 🚗 🚤 🏃
Cardwell, Lahood, Lewis & Clark Caverns, Willow Creek, Three Forks, Madison River Road, Quake Lake, West Yellowstone 🎣 ⛰ 🚗 🏃
Ruby River Scenic Drive ~ Twin Bridges, Ruby River Rd, Red Rock Lakes National Wildlife Refuge 🎣 ⛰ 🚗

A good Interactive Map: https://fwp.mt.gov/fishMT/explore

Lazy Boy Shop and Go Road Trip

Packing list for a road trip: chances are you have a fully stocked camper, but you may want to review the Raft list to be sure you haven't forgotten something necessary. Don't forget your camp chairs.

Breakfast

Croissants with ham egg and cheese, grapefruit juice

Frozen waffles, strawberries, whip cream,
heat and eat sausage links

Yogurt, toasted English Muffin, butter, cream cheese, sliced strawberries

Lunch or Snacks

Salami & Cheese Platter

Deli Sliced Turkey & Provolone cheese on Sourdough bread with tomato and Thousand Island Dressing

Deli Corned Beef, Pickles, Provolone Cheese
on Cocktail Rye Bread, Mustard

Friday Dinner

Thin Crust Pizza to Grill with Tomatoe Halves, Mozzarella Cheese, spray canola oil, alluminum foil

Saturday Dinner

Grilled Steak, foil roasted New Potatoes, Corn on the cob

Sunday Dinner

Chicken Gorgonzola Salad; Lettuce, Fully Cooked Chicken Breast ~ cubed, Gorgonzola cheese, Walnuts, Rasberry Vinagarette, Sourdough Bread ~ toasted with garlic butter

Desserts

Dark Chocolate and Sea Salt Caramels, Flathead Cherries

Beverges

Coffee, Tea, Orange Juice, Water, Soda, Beer, Wine, etc.

Recipe's for a Road Trip Shopping List

Avocado Toast 2 avocados Juice of 1 lime, Salt and pepper 1/2 cup crumbled feta cheese 2 Roma tomatoes, chopped 4 slices whole grain seedy bread ¼ cup butter, softened	page 159 Tools: griddle, spatula, mixing bowl, cutting board small knife
Pepper Jack Eggs 4 eggs 2 cups pepper jack cheese 4 corn tortillas 16 ounce can refried beans 2 tomatoes, diced 1 sweet onion, diced Green chili salsa Spray oil	page 162 Tools: 14 inch nonstick griddle, spatula, cooks gloves
Eggs Benedict 8 eggs 4 english muffins 8 slices Canadian style bacon 1.25 ounce pkg. Hollandaise Sauce Mix ½ cup Real Butter ¼ cup whipping cream 1 cup cold water 2 tsp Dijon Mustard Olive oil spray	page 166 Tools: high sided fry pan, small saucepan, alluminum foil, fork, slotted spoon
Cream Biscuits & Strawberry Butter 1 ½ cups Self Rising flour 3/4 cup whipping cream, not half and half 2 teaspoons sugar 1 tablespoon Crisco® shortening 1 pint fresh strawberries 3 teaspoons sugar ½ cup butter	Page 164

Rest Stop Rita's 2 large Spinach Tortillas 6 ounces thin sliced deli chicken ½ cup chipotle mayonnaise ½ cup plain yogurt 1 cup pepper jack cheese 1 cup shredded lettuce 1 tomato, chopped 1 avocado	page 167
Jeans Salmon Dip 7 ounce can pink salmon 8 ounces cream cheese 1 tablespoon minced onion 1 teaspoon horseradish 1 teaspoon Worcestershire sauce 1 dash liquid smoke 1 cup broken pecan pieces 8 ounce cracked pepper water crackers	Page 171 *2 - 6 people*
Rolling Roast Beef 10 inch flour tortilla 4 slices roast beef 2 slices cheddar cheese 2 slices monterey jack cheese ½ cup shredded lettuce ½ cup chopped tomato 2 tablespoons Honey Mustard or Horseradish Spray canola oil	page 169 *Per person*
Peanut Butter & Apple Chicken Wrap 3 slices deli style chicken breast ¼ apple thinly sliced 2 tablespoons crunchy peanut butter 1 taplesoon mayonnaise or greek yogurt 2 Romaine lettuce leaves	Page 167 Per person

Cajun New York & Ravioli 4 New York Strip Steaks 1/2 cup Worcestershire Sauce 2 tablespoons Franks® Red Hot Sauce 1 tablespoon brown sugar 1 tablespoon red wine vinegar Webers® N'Orleans Cajun Seasoning Coarse Ground Black Pepper olive oil , steak sauce 25 ounce bag frozen Ravioli 15 ounce can pizza sauce	**page 133** 4 people: Tools: large griddle or cast iron steak plates, tin plates, spatula
Hot and Spicy Asian Salad 2 large boneless skinless chicken breasts 2 Tablespoons Hot Chili Oil 2 Tablespoons olive oil 1 red onion 1 ounce package chicken taco seasoning 1 Tablespoon minced garlic 2 cups Asian sesame dressing 2 cups peanuts chopped cabbage or crispy mixed greens	page 195 4-6 people tools: 8 skewers sauce pan
Larry's Angel Hair Shrimp Gorgonzola 1 cup gorgonzola cheese 4 tablespoons butter 4 tablespoons olive oil 2 ounces fresh basil crumbled 3 tablespoons basil paste 1 tablespoon dried oregano flakes 12 ounces angel hair pasta 2 Roma tomatoes, chopped Fully cooked frozen shrimp, extra large 1 loaf sliced garlic bread	page 187 4 people tools: high sided fry pan, spatula, cutting board, slicing knife, aluminum foil
Days End Toasted Donuts, Rasberry jam Crispy Apple Flautas Campfire berries and cake	 page 204 page 206 page 208

Wake Up and Smell the Coffee

Avocado Toast
4 people ~ tools: griddle, spatula, mixing bowl, small sharp knife, cutting board

4 avocados
Juice of 1 lime, Salt and pepper
1 cup crumbled feta cheese
2 roma tomatoes, chopped
8 slices whole grain coody bread
¼ cup butter, softened

Peel and slice the avocado's. Mash in a bowl with salt, pepper and lime juice. Toast bread on griddle over hot coals. Spread generously with butter and avocado. Top with feta cheese and chopped tomato.

Last Night's Salmon on Toast
4 people ~ tools: griddle, spatula, mixing bowl, small sharp knife, cutting board

2 cups cooked flaked salmon
4 tablespoons chipotle mayonnaise
8 hamburger dill pickles, finely chopped
4 hardboiled eggs
8 slices whole grain bread
½ cup butter, softened

Mix salmon, chipotle mayo and chopped pickles together in a bowl. Slice eggs. Toast bread on the griddle over hot coals, flip and butter the toasted side. Top with egg slices and salmon spread.

Fruit Fried Oats
4 to 6 people ~ tools: 1 fry pan, serving spoon

8 ounce can pear chunks ~ no sugar added
8 ounce can mandarin oranges
1 cup dried cranberries or cherries
 ½ cup chopped walnuts
2 tablespoons brown sugar
¼ teaspoon cinnamon
1 cup old fashioned oats
¼ cup butter
2 single serving tubs vanilla yogurt

Mix butter and oats in a fry pan. Place on the grill over medium low coals and stir until oats crisp and brown a little. Add remaining ingredients to the pan, including the fruit juice. Stir once. Heat until mixture starts to bubble. Remove from heat and serve. Top with vanilla yogurt.

Breakfast Burrito
4-8 people ~ tools: 1 fry pan, spatula

8 eggs,
1 pound lean ground sausage *(Jimmy Dean is very lean)*
1 can refried beans *(we like Rosarita's fat free refried beans)*
8   flour tortilla's ~ thin style
1 12 ounce package shredded Mexican cheese
canola oil
1 8 ounce bottle mild taco sauce
Optional: hash browns (cooked in pan after sausage)

Crumble sausage into the fry pan and cook over medium hot coals, stirring to brown on all sides. Push sausage to the side of the pan and add refried beans. When the beans are warm, push them to the side of the pan opposite the sausage. Pour oil into the center of the pan and crack eggs into the pan and scramble. Top eggs with cheese. Spoon a little of everything onto each tortilla and wrap burrito style.

Huevos Rancheros
4 people ~ tools: 1 fry pan, spatula

4 eggs
1 pound chorizo sausage
1 can refried beans, we like Rosarita's fat free
4 squares tin foil
1 chopped tomato
1 can salsa
½ onion
4 warm tortillas
2 Tablespoons canola oil
Optional: Shredded Cheddar Cheese

Cook sausage in fry pan on the grill over a bed of hot coals.
Spread refried beans evenly over tortillas and place 1 tortillas
on each foil square. Top the tortilla with tomato and onion.
By now your sausage will be done so spoon sausage onto
the tortillas. Fold the tortilla in half. Fold the foil over the
tortilla and seal the edges. Set to the side of your grill to
warm.   Wipe pan with paper towel to remove excess
sausage grease. Put canola oil in pan then crack eggs into
the pan and cook "over easy".   Open the warmed tortillas.
Top with egg, salsa and optional: cheese.

Pepper Jack Eggs
4 people ~ tools: 14 inch non stick griddle, spatula
leather cooks gloves

4 eggs
2 cups pepper jack cheese, shredded
4 corn tortillas
16 ounce can refried beans, we like Rosarita's fat free
2 tomatoes, diced
1 sweet onion, diced
Green chili salsa
Spray oil

Grate pepper jack cheese, dice onion and tomato.
Open the refried beans.

Spray griddle with oil and place on grill over hot coals.
Spoon refried beans onto one side of the griddle and the
corn tortillas on the other side. Flip the beans once and slide
to the side of the grill. Stack the tortillas on top of the beans
to warm.

Spray oil on the empty side of the grill and sprinkle on the
diced onion. Sprinkle the shredded cheese on top of the
onion. When the cheese melts and begins to brown crack
the eggs onto the cheese. Cover with foil and cook until
egg whites are firm and egg yolks are slightly soft. Remove
from heat. Cheese will turn golden brown and the edges
crispy as it cools.

Spread refried beans on tortillas. Slide on the cheesy eggs.
Top with salsa.

Breakfast Pizza
4 people ~ tools: non-stick griddle or sheet pan, spatula

4 Naan Bread rounds
4 large eggs
1 tablespoon olive oil
2 tablespoons butter
Salt and pepper
2 beefsteak tomato's
2 cups fresh ricotta cheese drained
1 pound mozzarella cheese shredded
black olives

Heat griddle or large skillet over medium hot coals
Add a small splash of water to the pan and cook naans until
blisterd on the bottom. Flip and brown the other side.
Spread with butter. Top with ricotta, tomato and shredded
mozzarella. Heat until cheese is bubbly. Transfer to plates.

Pour a little olive oil into your warm frypan, crack eggs into
pan and fry sunny side up. Season with salt and pepper.
Serve one egg on each Naan Pizza.

Strawberry Butter and Cream Biscuits
6 biscuits ~ tools: mixing bowl, fry pan, spatula, aluminum foil

Biscuits
1 ½   cups self rising flour
3/4   cup whipping cream, *not half and half*
2   teaspoons sugar
1   Tablespoon Crisco® vegetable shortening

Strawberry Butter
1   pint fresh strawberries
3   teaspoons sugar
½ cup butter

Place flour into a mixing bowl or cook pot and stir in cream until dough forms. With floured hands kneed dough together until well mixed. Separate dough into 6 pieces and flatten to one inch thick. Grease the fry pan bottom and sides well. Warm the fry pan on the grill for a couple of minutes, not too hot, just warm to the touch. Place dough into pre-warmed greased frypan, Cover with aluminum foil and allow the dough to rise about 20 minutes. Bake over medium coals for about 10 minutes or until the bottoms start to brown.

While biscuits are resting, wipe out the dough bowl. Remove stems from the strawberries and slice into the bowl in 4 quarters. Sprinkle with sugar

When the bottom of the biscuits are light brown, arrange sliced strawberries around the sides of the pan and between the biscuits. Dot with butter. Gently lift the biscuits with a spatula so the strawberries and butter slide under the biscuits. Continue to cook about 5 minutes or until strawberries are hot. Remove from grill and serve with berries and butter topping the biscuits.

Another way to cook biscuits and quick breads without burning the bottom would be to use 2 disposable aluminum cake pans. Grease one pan with margarine. Arrange rolls in pan and seal the edges. Use the second foil pan like a double boiler. Arrange a handful of small rocks in the bottom of the pan and pour water into the pan to the top of the rocks. Place pan on the grill over medium hot coals. When the water is hot place the cake pan with the rolls on top of the rocks. Bake the biscuits about 15 minutes.

Quick Orange Nut Pull~A~Parts

4 people ~ tools: two 9 inch foil pans

6 brown and serve
  dinner rolls
¼ cup salted butter
¼ cup maple syrup
¼ cup dark brown sugar
1 cup broken walnut pieces
½ cup orange marmalade
12 ounce cream cheese frosting from the cake box isle.

Cut rolls in half top to bottom. Melt butter in pan over low coals. Stir in syrup, sugar, marmalade and nuts. Heat until bubbling, careful not to burn! Move to the side of the grill. Arrange rolls in the pan cut side down. Return to low heat for two to three minutes so rolls have time to absorb the syrup. Melt an additional tablespoon of butter in the second pan. Invert the rolls into the second pan so goodies are on top. Spread with frosting.

Eggs Benedict

4 people ~ tools: griddle or high sided fry pan,
small saucepan, alluminum foil, fork, slotted spoon

8 eggs
4 english muffins
8 slices Canadian style bacon
1 ounce package Hollandaise Sauce Mix
½ cup salted sweet cream Butter
¼ cup whipping cream (saved from your coffee)
1 cup cold water
2 tsp Dijon Mustard
Olive oil spray

Melt ½ stick butter in saucepan over medium coals. Stir in water and sauce mix. Whisk with a fork until mix is completely dissolved. Stir in Cream and Mustard. Cook over medium coals, stirring constantly until sauce starts to boil. Move pan to the edge of grill to simmer. Stir occasionally until mix begins to thicken. Set aside.

Split muffins in half and spray with olive oil. Toast on a doubled sheet of foil on the grill over medium hot coals, being careful not to burn them. Meanwhile, Warm Canadian Bacon on a large square of foil that has been sprayed with oil. Spread ½ of the butter on toasted muffins, put them on the foil with the bacon and set to side of grill to keep warm.

Pour 3 inches of water into the fry pan. Place on the grill over low flames to boil. Adjust heat so water continues to simmer.

Carefully crack each egg into a small cup without breaking the yolk and slip the egg into the simmering water. Cook eggs until whites are completely set and yolks begin to thicken but are not hard 3-5 minutes. Do Not Stir! Lift eggs out of the water with slotted spoon, drain well. Top each muffin with Bacon, Egg and 2 tablespoons sauce.

Easy No Meat Frittata

4 people ~ tools: sheet pan or large fry pan, spatula

3 Tablespoons olive oil
3 green onions, chopped
8 ounces fresh mushrooms, sliced
1 can corn, drained of water
1 green pepper, chopped
1 can sliced black olives
6 eggs
1 teaspoon chili powder
salt & pepper
1 tomato, chopped
1 cup grated cheddar cheese
salsa, optional

Warm oil in fry pan over medium coals. Saute' onions and mushrooms, add corn and green pepper. Pour eggs into the pan. Sprinkle on chili powder salt and pepper. Cover the pan and move to low heat about 8 inches above the coals. Serve when eggs are nearly firm and before they become overcooked and dry.

Off the Road Breaks and Apps
Take time to smell the flowers

Rest Stop Rita's

2 large Spinach Tortillas
6 ounces thin sliced deli chicken
½ cup chipotle mayonnaise
½ cup plain yogurt
1 cup shredded pepper jack cheese
1 cup shredded lettuce
1 tomato, chopped
1 avocado, peeled, pitted and diced

Mix chipotle mayonnaise and yogurt together with the cheese. Divide the chicken between the tortillas. Spread with Chipotle Cheese sauce, Top with lettuce tomato and avocado. Roll up. Cut into 4 slices each.

Peanut Butter & Apple Chicken Wrap
For each serving

3 slices deli style chicken breast
½ apple thinly sliced
2 Tablespoons crunchy peanut butter
1 Tabllesoon lite mayonnaise or greek yogurt
2 Romaine lettuce leaves

Separate lettuce leaves. Spread each piece of lettuce with peanut butter all the way to the edges. Stick the lettuce together side by side with the peanut butter. Top one side of the lettuce with chicken, spread on a little mayo for the juicy effect, then add the apple slices. Roll it up so the second piece of lettuce holds the apples in with the peanut butter.

Tiny Torta's
4-6 people ~ tools: Slicing knife, fry pan, fork

6 small French Dinner Rolls
Butter or margarine
6 slices Canadian bacon
1 medium avocado
Lime juice & salt
6 slices jack cheese
½ cup shredded lettuce
2 tsp Red or green salsa

Split rolls, spread with butter and grill buttered side until
toasted, saute bacon, mash together avocado lime and salt
Top toasted rolls with Canadian bacon, cheese avocado
mix, lettuce, and salsa. Serve immediately.

Asian Lettuce Wrap
4-6 people ~ tools: large bowl, small bowl or cup

1 deli roasted chicken, meat removed and shredded
½ cup shredded carrots
1 8 ounce can sliced water chestnuts, drained & chopped
½ cup plain yogurt
½ cup Asian dressing and marinade
1 head Boston or Bibb lettuce

Mix chicken, carrots and water chestnuts in a large bowl.
In a smaller bowl or cup, stir yogurt and Asian dressing
together until smooth. Pour over chicken mixture and toss to
coat.

Spoon chicken mixture onto lettuce leaves and wrap.

Rolling Roast Beef
Per person ~ tools: non-stick aluminum foil, knife

10 inch flour tortilla
4 thin slices roast beef
2 slices cheddar cheese
2 slices provolone cheese
½ cup shredded lettuce
½ cup chopped tomato
2 Tablespoons Honey Mustard or Horseradish
Spray canola oil

Spray the **shiny** side of your aluminum foil with cooking oil
and place a tortilla on it. Spread with honey mustard. Top
with cheese first, then roast beef. Fold in half and wrap up
tightly in the foil. Put it in a secure place under the hot hood
of your truck. Not in a hurry? The hot dashboard also works.
Take a walk … go fishing.

Unwrap warmed tortilla and add lettuce and tomato.

*Or if you happen to be packing a camper equipped with a
microwave?   Place tortilla on a plate cover with cheese and
roast beef. Microwave for 30 seconds or until cheese is
melted. Spread with mustard, Top with lettuce and tomato.*

Gramma used to cook a whole chicken dinner under the
hood of the car driving from Butte to Lewistown. But before
you try to do this be sure to read more about it on the
internet. Some sources of information are:

Wikihow: cooking with your cars engine
You Tube: doityourself.com

Marinated Olives & Cheese Crostini
4 people ~ tools: paper bowl, knife, plate, plastic wrap

4 ounce package garlic and herb goat cheese
¼ cup white wine
½ cup finely chopped marinated olives
1 tablespoon olive oil
10 ounce package crostini

Soften cheese to room temperature or about 65 degrees. Mix goat cheese and wine together to the consistency of a soft cream cheese. Mold into soft round and cover with plastic wrap. Place in the cooler for 1 hour to 4 days.

Drizzle olive oil on a pretty plate. Place mound of cheese in the center of the plate and top with chopped olives. Surround with warmed crostini. Serve with a small knife.

Gorgonzola Dip
Serve with bread sticks or crackers

At Home:

1 8 ounce package cream cheese
1 5 ounce package crumbled gorgonzola cheese
1 cup sour cream
small sprinkle of garlic seasoning
8 ounce package medium size breadsticks
   or crackers

Put cream cheese in a glass bowl and soften in the microwave for 30 seconds on high. Stir in sour cream and gorgonzola cheese. Transfer to tight sealing refrigerator container and refrigerate several hours or overnight. Add a little milk or more sour cream if you want a thinner dip.

Jean's Salmon Dip

1 cup last nights cooked salmon, chopped
   or 7 ounce can pink salmon
8 ounces cream cheese
1 Tablespoon minced onion
1 teaspoon horseradish
1 teaspoon Worcestershire sauce
1 dash liquid smoke
1 cup broken pecan pieces

Warm cream cheese to room temperature. Chop fresh cooked salmon or drain all liquid from canned salmon and dry with paper towel. Mix well with softened cream cheese, onion, horseradish, Worcestershire and liquid smoke. Cover and put in the cooler for at least an hour to allow seasoning to blend. Top with pecans before serving with crackers.

Green Chili Cheese Dip

8   ounces Velveeta® Cheese
2   Tblespoons butter
7 ounce can chopped green chilis
½ cup sour cream

At Home: Place Velveeta® Cheese and butter in the microwave for one minute or only until it is melted enough to stir. Stir in chopped green chilis and sour cream. Store in plastic bowl with a tight lid. This is a good served hot or cold. Serve with tortilla chips.

Grilled Feta Dip

1 Tablespoon margarine
8 ounces softened cream cheese
7 ounces crumbled Feta Cheese, Mediterranean Herb
7 ounce can sliced black olives

Spread margarine and cream cheese in an aluminum foil pie pan over low coals. Top with feta and olives, warm on grill over medium coals until melted.
Serve with Rosemary and Olive Oil Crackers

Crab Tornado

6 people ~ tools: mixing bowl, cutting board, knife, spoon,
6 squares of non-stick aluminum foil

8 ounce package imitation crab meat
8 ounce package cream cheese, softened
2 finely chopped green onion
2 finely chopped roma tomatoes
8 ounce package crumbled gorgonzola cheese
1 Tablespoon ground black pepper
Package of 6 mini French rolls ~ 4 inches
½ cup butter or margarine
Spray cooking oil

Mix together the cream cheese, onion, tomato, gorgonzola and pepper. Slice crab meat into one inch lengths and separate into stringy pieces in the mixing bowl. Fold into cream cheese mix.

Spray foil with cooking oil. Slice rolls in half and butter the inside halves. Fill generously with Crab mix. Spray outside of bread roll with oil to assist non burning. Roll up in foil and place on the grill over medium coals until heated through. Turn often.

Ham and Cheese Pull Apart

4-8 people ~ tools: non-stick aluminum foil, cutting board, serrated knife, forks

1 16 ounce loaf Italian or Sourdough Bread
½ cup margarine, Not water added margarine
16 ounces chopped ham
8 ounces pepper jack cheese, cubed
8 ounces medium cheddar cheese, cubed
1 4 ounce can chopped green chilis
Spray canola oil

Spray all sides of the bread with oil. Cut bread in a grid pattern, about one inch between rows. Do not cut through the bottom crust so the bread remains slightly together.

Place two 24 inch pieces of foil across each other on a flat surface (like a cross). Carefully place the bread in the center of the foil keeping the bread together.

Spread softened margarine between bread pieces. Stuff ham, cheese and chilis between bread pieces, the more the better. Wrap foil around bread and seal the edges.

Place upside down on grill over medium coals for 5 to 10 minutes to start the cheese melting. Turn and heat the bottom side for another 10 minutes or until cheese melts into the bread.   Pull apart with fingers or forks.

Grilled Nectarine & Cheese Crostini

4-6 people ~ tools: sheet pan, spoon, spatula, leather gloves

1 french bread baguette
½ cup balsamic vinegar
2 tablespoon olive oil
8 ounce softened goat cheese, sliced
2 nectarines

Slice nectarines into 6 slices each. Place on grill over hot coals for 45 second each side. Remove to plate.

Slice baguette into 10 or 12 pieces. Place sheet pan on grill over hot coals. Drizzle olive oil on sheet pan. Stir vinegar into oil and allow to simmer for a minute to mix. Place baguette slices onto the pan and turn each piece to coat both sides. Toast one side, flip. Top with a slice of cheese and nectarine. Allow cheese to warm slightly before serving.

Thai Skewered Shrimp

Per serving ~ wood or metal skewers

4 Extra Large Shrimp, peeled, deveined, rinsed and dried
Lemon juice
Lemon pepper
Spicy Thai dipping sauce and marinade

Skewer shrimp and sprinkle with lemon juice and pepper. drizzle with olive oil. Place on grill over hot coals, about two to three minutes per side or until no longer transparent and slightly pink. Drizzle with Thai sauce.

Note: wooden skewers should be soaked in water before using so they don't burn

Cheese and Olive on Rye
6 people ~ tools: aluminum foil, medium size bowl

1½ cups cheddar cheese, grated
1   cup chopped black olives
2   cups dried chipped beef
¾ cup mayonnaise
1 loaf sliced party rye bread

Mix cheese, olives, chipped beef and mayonnaise in a medium size bowl. Spray a sheet of aluminum foil with oil. Foil should be 6 inches longer than the loaf of bread. Place bread on foil and spread mix between bread slices. Wrap tightly and seal edges. Place on grill over medium low coals to warm. Turn occasionally.

Dublin Nachos
6 people ~ tools: Sheet pan, spatula, slicing knife, gloves

22 ounce bags frozen steak fries
2 pounds thick sliced corned beef
8 ounces shredded cheddar cheese
8 ounces shredded pepper jack cheese
1 8 ounce can chopped green chilis
1 large tomato
1 eight ounce can sliced black olives
Salt and pepper
Canola Oil ~ Optional: sour cream, green chili salsa

Pour a thin coating of oil onto a sheet pan and place it on the grill over hot coals. Cut potatoes into bite size pieces and spread them out over the hot oil. Salt and pepper the potatoes. Flip as needed to avoid burning.

Chop corned beef into small chunks and toss in with the potatoes. When the potatoes and corned beef are crispy top with cheese, green chilies, diced tomato, and olives.

The Main Event

Charcoal Grilled Chicken Breast

Bone on is much juicer and tender cooked on the grill than Boneless.

Baste with olive oil or marinade. Place chicken pieces, bone side down about 5 inches from medium hot coals. Cook 30 to 40 minutes, turn and cook another 20 to 30 minutes basting with sauce frequently.

Consider sauces made with
Lemon and Garlic or Honey and Oranges.

Charcoal Grilled Steak

Trim any excess fat from the steak and slash the remaining fat at two inch intervals to keep the sides from curling up. Place steak on the grill four inches from hot coals. Season after turning.

One inch thick steak	Two inch thick steak
Rare: 4 to 5 minutes per side	Rare: 12 to 13 minutes per side
Medium: 7 to 8 minutes per side	Medium: 15 to 17 minutes per side
Well: 10 to 11 minutes per side	Well: 22 to 25 minutes per side

How you slice your meat matters.

Slice against the grain for tenderness.
With the grain is only for things like pulled pork or chicken.

Baked Potatoes
Tools: leather gloves to turn potatoes

1 potato per person
Canola Oil
Heavy aluminum foil
Salt and pepper
Butter
Sour cream

Scrub Potatoes and pierce with a fork to allow steam to escape, then rub with oil. Wrap in heavy aluminum foil. Place on grill three inches from the coals and cook about an hour turning frequently. You can also place them directly in the coals but you still need to turn them frequently and they will still take 50 to 60 minutes to bake.

Stroganoff Potato
4 people ~ tools: high sided fry pan, spatula, slicing knife paper plates, aluminum foil

4 previously baked potatoes
1½ pound lean hamburger
8 ounces sliced mushrooms
10 ounce can beefy gravy
3 Tablespoons butter
1 cup sour cream

Cut each potato half way through and wrap in foil. Place on grill to heat, rolling occasionally so as not to burn. Crumble hamburger into high sided fry pan and cook over hot coals until no longer pink. Drain any grease. Add sliced mushrooms and butter to the frypan and saute' over hot coals until mushrooms brown. Add gravy and stir frequently until gravy bubbles. Remove from heat and gently stir in Sour Cream. Open center of hot baked potato and fluff insides. Spoon stroganoff mix onto the potatoes.

Potato's with Bean Gravy

2 people ~ tools: aluminum foil, tin plates, small sauce pan knife & forks, leather cooks gloves

2 previously baked potatoes
15 ounce can Bush's Best White Chili Beans
     in Mild Chili Sauce
2 tablespoons butter, salt & pepper

Slice potatoes in half and wrap in foil. Heat on grill over hot coals, turning occasionally. Pour the can of beans into pan and place on grill over hot coals. Stir occasionally until heated through. Spoon onto hot potatoes.
Top with butter

Baby Potatoes for a Crowd

*10-12 people ~ tools: Large Canning Pot with lid,
        Leather Gloves, Large slotted spoon.*

5 pound bag of baby red and/or yukon gold potatoes
1 gallon of water, approximately
Olive oil, Salt
Butter
Sour cream

Fill cook pot ½ full with water. Place on low grill over hot coals. Cover pot and bring water to a boil. Rinse potatoes and add to boiling water. Cover and cook about 20 minutes
Potatoes should be firm but forkable. Remove from heat. Potatoes will continue to cook in the hot water. Drain water when you are ready to eat. Serve with butter and sour cream.

Benton Road Dinner for a crowd

12 people ~ tools: 2 large cookpots,
long handle serving spoon

3 pounds boneless pork tenderloin
3 pounds smoked brats or kielbasa
3 pounds fully cooked ham steak
1 28 ounce can chili beans
1 28 ounce can black beans
1 28 ounce can great northern beans
12 ounce can chicken broth
3 family size Boil In Bag White Rice about 16 ounces
2 16 ounce bottles of water
½ pound butter

Cut pork, brats and ham into large bite size pieces. Pour enough oil into a large cookpot to coat the bottom of the pan. Place on grill over low flame. Add pork pieces to the pan first and allow to brown for a minute, add the brats to brown then ham. Stir occasionally until all meat is fully cooked.

Add beans and broth to the pot of meat. Allow to simmer at least 30 minutes and up to an hour.   Add water if necessary, you will want a juicy mix to top your rice ~ juicy not soupy.

For Rice: In second pot bring water to a boil over low flame. Completely submerge rice in the boiling water and boil 8 minutes. Remove pot from heat. Pour rice into a large serving dish. Dot with butter. Spoon Meat and Beans over the rice.

Serve with grilled corn on the cob.

Grilled Corn on the Cob
Tools: leather gloves to turn corn

1 ear of corn per person, *plus 2 for Tomorrow's Corn Salad
Olive oil
1 tablespoons butter for each ear of corn
Aluminum foil
Salt and pepper

Peel back corn husks and remove silk. Drizzle each piece with oil, lightly salt and pepper. Close husks. Wrap each ear of corn tightly in foil. Place on grill over hot coals. Cook about 30 minutes turning occasionally until corn is tender. Serve with butter.

With a sharp knife scrape the leftover corn off the cob into a quart size seal tight plastic bag. Put into the cooler.

Tomorrow's Corn Salad
4 people ~ tools: seal tight plastic bag, can opener, knife, cutting board

2 ears of leftover grilled corn, sliced from the cob
1 red bell pepper, and/or ½ red onion
1 15 ounce can black beans
1 6 ounce can sliced black olives
2 tablespoons lime juice
¼ cup fresh cilantro leaves
Salt

Lightly salt leftover corn in the seal tight plastic bag. Chop red pepper and onion into small pieces and add to corn. Drain and rinse black beans, add to corn. Drain olives and add to corn. Add chopped green chilies and cilantro. Seal and tip side to side to blend ingredients.

Inverness Fettuccini & Tenderloin Whisky Cream Sauce

4 people ~ tools: saucepan, high sided frypan, sharp knife, serving spoon

8 ounces fettucine noodles
3 pounds boneless tenderloin roast or steak
Olive oil
1 small onion, diced
8 mushrooms, chopped
½ cup whiskey
1 cup beef broth
½ cup heavy whipping cream
2 cups shredded sharp white cheese, like Coastal

Bring 4 cups water to a boil in medium size saucepan. Add one tablespoon olive oil and the pasta. Cook over hot coals until pasta is tender but a little firm. Move to the side of the grill.

Cut tenderloin into ½ inch thick medallions.

Coat the bottom of a skillet with oil and place on grill over medium hot coals. Add the onions and mushrooms until browned. Add steak and sear on both sides. **Remove pan from the grill** and pour in the whiskey. *Do not pour whiskey into pan on the grill or you could burn yourself.*

When the whiskey evaporates slide steak to the side of the pan and stir in the beef broth and cream. Return to the grill. Stir until liquid starts to bubble, move to the side of the grill to keep warm and stir in cheese until melted.

Drain any remaining liquid from the pasta. Divide onto plates and top with hot steak and sauce.

Pork Tenderloin with Roasted Red Potatoes, Cob Corn
8 people ~ tools: aluminum foil

4 pound pork tenderloin roast
8 medium sized red potatoes
8 corn on the cob
cooking oil
butter
sour cream
salt & Pepper
steak sauce

Pull back the husk of the corn and remove the silk. Leave
the husk on the corn and soak in a tub of water while you
prepare a fire with plenty of coals. Pierce potatoes with a
fork and place each on a small square of aluminum foil
drizzle with cooking oil and wrap tightly in foil. Place
potatoes on the grill over hot coals to bake. Remove corn
from the water and allow to drip dry before placing them on
the grill. Turn potatoes and corn often to keep from
scorching. Cook about 40 minutes or until potatoes feel soft.
Move corn to each side of the grill and stack the potatoes on
top of the corn. Replenish the coals under the center of your
grill before placing your pork roast in the center of the grill.
Brush cooking oil over the roast and grill barbeque style.
Turning often until pork is no longer pink in the middle. Serve
with butter, sour cream, salt and pepper.

Italian Pork Chops with Spaghetti

4 people ~ tools: 1 large frypan, aluminum foil, spatula, can opener

4 boneless center cut pork chops
2 tablespoons canola oil
½ cup red wine
1 can Italian seasoned crushed tomatoes
1 tablespoon Italian seasoning
½ teaspoon minced garlic

1 cup water
½ package of thin spaghetti noodle
1 chopped green pepper
1 chopped onion
1 pkg sliced mushroom

Prepare campfire until you have a bed of hot coals. Heat oil in large frypan. Add pork chops. Sear meat on both sides. Add red wine, tomatoes, seasoning and cover with foil. Slide pan to the side of coals to allow the ingredients to simmer slowly until pork chops are tender.

Remove the foil cover and place on the side of the grill. Place pork chops on top of the foil. Pour water into the pan and heat until sauce is bubbly, add spaghetti noodles, lift pork chops on top of noodles with a fork. Top with peppers onion and mushrooms. Cover and simmer until noodles are tender. Remove from heat.

Serve with Garlic Bread

Purchase garlic bread in foil wrapper. Simply warm bread in the wrapper on the side of the grill while you are cooking.

Quick Three Way Sauce
Red Spaghetti, Pizza, Tomato Soup
Makes aproximately 2 quarts

Prepare at home, Cool and pack in seal tight freezer bags.

8 large ripe tomatoes
1 green bell pepper
1 yellow bell pepper
1 sweet onion
2 stalks celery
1 cups chicken broth
3 Tbs butter
1 tsp sugar

Chop peppers onion and celery into tiny pieces and sauté with butter in a medium size saucepot. Cut the tomatoes in half and puree in the blender. Pour the tomatoes into the saucepot with the vegetables. Add Chicken broth and seasoning. Simmer on medium low heat for 45 minutes. Cool, Pack into two quart size seal tight freezer bags. Freeze for camping.

Pizza
4 people ~ tools: large fry pan or pancake griddle, spatula

1 large Boboli Bread
1 ½ cups Three Way Sauce
8 ounces freshly grated mozzarella cheese
1 teaspoon Italian seasoning
olive oil
optional; pepperoni, black olives, diced tomato, bell peppers

Brush bottom of the Boboli Bread with oil and place in pan. Spread on sauce, sprinkle on seasoning. Arrange cheese and any additional ingredients on top evenly. Place pan on grill over medium hot coals. Cover with foil until cheese is melted.

Spaghetti
4-6 people ~ tools: 2 medium size cook pots, tin plate, paper towels, large long handled serving spoon

1 pound extra lean ground Italian sausage
3 cups Three Way Sauce
14 ounce package thin spaghetti
1 teaspoon italian seasoning
½ teaspoon garlic juice or seasoning to taste
olive oil
freshly grated parmesan cheese

Pour a small amount of olive oil in the bottom of one pot. Crumble in the sausage and cook over hot coals, stirring often. Move to the side of the grill. Wipe out any excess grease with a paper towel and add Three Way Sauce. Allow to simmer over medium low coals.

Add 6 cups water to the second pot and boil over hot coals or low flames. Break dry spaghetti in half and add to boiling water. Boil 8 to 10 minutes or until pasta is tender (Add water a cup at a time if necessary to maintain water over the top of noodles.) Drain any excess water.
Serve with toasted Garlic Bread

Tomato Soup
4 people/ tools: large cook pot, soup ladel, aluminum foil

4 cups Three Way Sauce
2 cups chicken broth
1 teaspoon crushed rosemary
½ cup whipping cream
6 ounces freshly grated parmesan
Toasted Baguette
Olive oil, Itallian or garlic and herb seasoning

Mix three way sauce and chicken broth in the cook pot. Heat on grill over medium hot coals stirring often until soup starts to simmer. Move to the side of the grill. Stir in Whipping Cream. Top each serving of soup with fresh parmesan. Serve with Toasted Baguette.

Larry's Shrimp & Angel Hair Gorgonzola

6 people ~ tools: high sided fry pan, spatula, cutting board, slicing knife, aluminum foil

1 cup gorgonzola cheese, crumbled
4 tablespoons butter
4 tablespoons olive oil
2 ounces fresh basil crumbled
3 tablespoons basil paste
1 tablespoon dried oregano flakes
Salt and pepper
12 ounces angel hair pasta
2 romano tomatoes, chopped
2 pounds frozen cooked jumbo shrimp

1 loaf sliced garlic bread purchased in foil wrapper

Place garlic bread on the side of the grill to warm slowly, turn occasionally.

Fill frypan ½ full of water and add a few drops of olive oil. Bring water to a boil on grill over low flame or hot coals. Break pasta in half and add to boiling water. Cook one to two minutes or until pasta is barely tender. Remove from heat and drain water. Drizzle a little more oil over the pasta. Form a little boat with aluminum foil and slide pasta into the foil. Seal and set to the side of the grill to stay hot.

Pour 2 tablespoons of oil into the fry pan and place on grill over hot coals. Add shrimp. Season with basil, oregano, salt pepper and butter. Heat shrimp through. Blend in the cooked pasta and gorganzola. Top with chopped tomato. Serve immediately.

Rosemary Chicken and Vegetables

4 people ~ tools: 1 high sided fry pan, large serving spoon

4 boneless skinless chicken breasts
2 Tablespoons canola oil
1 pound carrots: cleaned and cut into ½ inch slices
1 head cauliflower: cleaned and cut into bite size chunks
1 cup chicken broth
¼ cup brown sugar
1 tablespoon chopped rosemary

Pour oil into the frypan and heat over medium hot coals. Add chicken breasts to the hot oil and sear on both sides to brown and seal in juices. Add carrots, sugar and rosemary to the pan, lifting chicken above the carrots. Allow carrots to caramelize in sugar and rosemary for about five minutes while stirring and gradually adding chicken broth as needed so the sugar does not burn. Add cauliflower to the pan, again lifting the chicken above the vegetables. Add remaining chicken broth and simmer until vegetables are tender and chicken is done.

Chips Fried Chicken

2-4 people ~ tools: 1 large high sided frypan

2 boneless skinless chicken breasts
8 ounce bag sour cream and onion flavored potato chips
1 egg
½ cup canola oil

Eat half the bag of chips while you prepare your fire. Crush the remaining chips in the bag. Crush well .. almost dust. Slice each chicken breast in half lengthwise so they are half as thick. Crack egg into quart size plastic bag and squish to mix. Put chicken pieces into eggs then into the bag of crushed chips. Shake it up. Heat Oil in fry pan over hot coals. Drop chicken into hot oil until browned. Flip once and brown on the other side.

Brian's Shrimp Table

6 people ~ tools: large cook pot, slicing knife, large slotted spoon, cooks leather gloves, garbage bags, folding table.

18 baby red and yellow potatoes
6 ears corn, each cut crosswise into 4 pieces
4 pounds extra-large shrimp, peeled and deveined
2 pounds fully cooked Andouille Sausage
Salt and Pepper
¼ pound Butter, Shrimp Sauce, Catsup, Mustard
Sliced Watermelon makes this a perfect meal

Fill a large pot halfway with water. Place on grill over low flame. When water starts to boil add corn and potatoes. Cook about 10 minutes or until potatoes can be pierced with a fork. Slice sausage into bite size pieces. Add sausage and shrimp to the boil pan. Continue to cook until shrimp is firm and pink. Drain all water. Cover a folding table with a large plastic garbage bag. Dump the entire pot onto the bag. Season with salt pepper, melted butter. Eat with fingers. Dip in sauces. Easy clean up, turn garbage bag inside out with mess inside. *Brian and Bria made enough for 20 people and it was delicious.*

Dearborn River

Sheet Pan Chicken Fajitas

4 – 6 people ~ tools: high sided sheet pan, slicing knife, large serving spoon, cutting board, cooks leather gloves, aluminum foil

2 boneless skinless Chicken Breasts
1 ounce package chicken fajita seasoning mix
½ cup water
1 each Red, Yellow and Green Bell Peppers
1 medium onion
1 or 2 limes
3 tablespoons chopped cilantro
8 flour tortillas
12 ounce package shredded Mexican Cheese blend
Olive oil
Optional: chipotle ranch dressing or sour cream,
             sliced avocado, sliced tomato

Spray tortillas with oil and wrap in foil. Warm on the outside edge of the grill. Turn occasionally.

Slice chicken into thin strips and sprinkle with fajita seasoning mix. Peel onion and slice into thin strips. Slice peppers into strips, discarding seeds and stems.

Drizzle sheet pan with oil and place on grill over hot coals. Spread cut chicken onto the hot pan. Turn once when chicken looks about half done. *If necessary, Sprinkle with water to add moisture to the chicken.*

Add onion and peppers to the pan, drizzle with a little oil and lime juice. Toss with cilantro, salt and pepper as desired. When chicken is cooked through, and veggies are tender. (about 20 minutes altogether) divide fajita filling among tortillas. Top with cheese and optional ingredients.

Wicked Good Veggies

6 people ~ tools: sheet pan, large serving spoon, aluminum foil

12 ounce package Carrots, Cauliflower, Broccoli Mix
from the produce isle
8 Baby red and yellow new potatoes
Salt and Pepper
1 teaspoon dried Rosemary seasoning
1 cup Freshly grated Romano or Parmesan cheese
¼ cup Olive Oil
¼ cup Butter

Clean and cut potatoes in half or quarters depending on size. Place sheet pan on grill over hot coals. Drizzle with olive oil. Arrange the potatoes evenly on the pan in the hot oil. Sprinkle with salt and pepper and cook until potatoes are tender and lightly brown, turn once. Add veggie mix, drizzle with oil again and sprinkle rosemary seasoning over all. Cover with foil and continue cooking until veggies are hot and tender. Turn occasionally. Top with slices of butter, sprinkle with salt and pepper and cheese, serve when cheese melts.

Lemon Green Beans

4 people ~ tools: large saucepan or high sided fry pan, slotted spoon

1 pound fresh green beans
4 tablespoons butter
1 lemon
½ teaspoon lemon pepper

Fill pot with water and bring to boil over hot coals. Remove any dried ends from beans. Cut beans in half and submerge in boiling water for about 7 minutes or until tender crisp. Drain water. Top with butter and sprinkle on lemon pepper.

Mexican Menu
Stuffed Jalapenos, Chimichanga's,
Crispy Apple Flautas pg. 203

Pico De Gallo
Serve on chimichangas makes about 2 cups
tools: mixing bowl, knife, cutting board, serving spoon

2 medium tomatoes, chopped
1 large ear of fresh corn, sliced from the cob
1/ 4 cup fresh cilantro leaves
2 finely chopped green onions
2 Tablespoons lime juice
1/4 teaspoon salt

Mix all ingredients in bowl. Cover and place in cooler for an hour or more to allow flavors to mingle.

Stuffed Jalapenos
Serve as an appetizer
4 people ~ tools: sheetpan, non-stick aluminum foil,
sharp knife, spatula, tin plate

8 fresh Jalapeno Peppers
4 ounces cream cheese
½ cup shredded cheddar cheese
2 Tablespoons cooking oil

Slice peppers lengthwise on the tin plate and remove ALL seeds and membrane. Caution: do not to touch your face after handling pepper seeds, wash your hands. Mix together cheddar and cream cheese. Fill peppers with mix.

Line pan with foil and drizzle with oil. Arrange peppers on foil and place pan on grill over medium hot coals. Cook peppers until the bottom is roasted and cheese is melted.

Chimichanga's

4 people ~ tools: sheetpan, can opener, spatula, tin plate

1 ½ pounds ground beef
      or other cooked and shredded meat
1 can Rosarita's® fat free refried beans
½ pound sliced pepperjack cheese
4 large flour tortilla's
½ cup cooking oil
8 oz of shredded Mexican blend cheese
1 4 ounce can sliced black olives
Pico De Galo or green chili salsa
sour cream

Crumble ground beef into fry pan and cook over hot coals.
Wipe out any grease with a paper towel. Mix in refried
beans and divide evenly onto flour tortillas. Top with sliced
cheese. Fold the ends of the filled tortillas over the mix, then
roll one side to the other side so the ends are tucked in.
Wipe out your frypan.

Place chimichangas folded side down in oil that has been
heated over medium hot coals. Be carefull not to splatter oil
into flames. Brown lightly and turn over to brown the other
side. Transfer to hot tin plate and top with cheese, olives,
salsa, sour cream.

Chorizo and Potatoes

4 people ~ tools: 1 large non stick frypan, 1 medium size cookpot with lid, spatula and sharp knife, cutting board

4 large flour tortilla's
16 ounce bag frozen roasted potatoes
½ cup water
1 chopped tomato
1 diced green pepper
½ onion diced
1 pound ground chorizo sausage,
½ cup canola oil
1 12 oz package shredded cheddar cheese,
Serve with black olives, shredded lettuce, salsa, sour cream

Pour a tablespoon of oil in the bottom of the frypan and place over medium hot coals. Add the potatoes and water and cover. Cook until tender enough to mash with a fork, 10 to 15 minutes.

Put chorizo sausage in cook pot and break up into small pieces. Cook like taco meat, over medium hot coals. Drain grease from the sausage. Chop onion, pepper and tomatoes and sauté for a few minutes with the sausage.

Potato's should be ready, so mash them up with a fork. Mix potatoes into the sausage pot.

Pour ½ cup of oil into the frypan to heat over medium coals.

Spoon sausage potato mix onto tortilla's and fold in half. Put folded tortilla's into fry pan 2 at a time until brown and crisp on each side. Serve with additional toppings as desired.

Shrimp Tacos

4 -6 people ~ tools: wooden skewers, aluminum foil, spoon

26 to 30 large frozen shrimp, peeled and deveined
lemon juice
8 corn tortillas
2 cups cotija cheese
2 cups salsa
cooked cucumber avacado rice: recipe below

Soak wooden skewers in water so they don't burn. Spray tortillas with cooking oil and wrap them in alluminum foil. Put them on the grill to warm, turn occassionally. Thread about 6 shrimp on each skewer and drizzle with lemon juice. Place on the grill over medium hot coals. Turning often. Fill each tortilla with cooked rice and shrimp. Top with cheese and salsa.

Cucumber and Avocado Rice

4 people ~ tools: large saucepan or frypan, fork, spoon

1 ½ cups long grain white rice
2 cups water
½ cup lime juice (about 3 limes)
1 large seedless cucumber, chopped
1 ripe avacado chopped
 ½ cup fresh cilantro, chopped
 ¼ cup olive oil

Bring water to a boil in a large saucepan. Add 1 tablespoon olive oil and lime juice to the water. Stir in rice and cover. Cook about 20 minutes over medium coals until rice is tender but not mushy. Fluff rice with a fork and add cucumber, avacado and cilantro and remaining olive oil. Toss lightly.

Hot and Spicy Asian Chicken Salad

*4 – 6 people ~ tools: 8 skewers, medium size sauce pan
(if using wooden skewers, soak in water for 10 minutes)*

2 large boneless skinless chicken breasts
2 Tablespoons Hot Chili Oil
2 Tablespoons olive oil
1 red onion, cut into small squares and separated
1 Tablespoon minced garlic
1 ounce package chicken taco seasoning mix
1 ½ cups water
2 cups Asian sesame dressing
2 cups peanuts
16 ounce package cole slaw mix with shredded carrots

Heat olive oil in the saucepan on the grill over medium coals.
Add onion and garlic. Saute' until onion is tender, about one
minute. Mix together taco seasoning mix and water. Add to
saucepan and cook another minute to thicken the sauce.
Add Asian sesame dressing and peanuts. Set to side of the
grill to keep warm.

Cut chicken breast into large bite size pieces. Thread onto
skewers and brush with hot chili oil. Grill over medium hot
coals turning often. Serve over cole slaw mix and top with
spicy Asian dressing.

**Oars
+
Tarp
+
Rope
= Shelter**

Peanut and Sesame Noodles Chicken

4 – 6 people ~ tools: 1 large saucepan, 1 small saucepan or large tin coffee cup, large spoon with holes to strain water

1 fully cooked rotisserie chicken, shredded
1 pound spaghetti noodles
1/3 cup creamy peanut butter
1/4 cup low sodium soy sauce
2 Tablespoon sesame oil
1/2 teaspoon Siracha hot chili sauce
1 red bell pepper, thinly sliced
2 Tablespoons olive oil

AT HOME:
Shred chicken and wrap in alluminum foil, store in seal tight plastic bag. Freeze

IN CAMP:
Place thawed chicken in foil on the side of the grill to warm. Turn ocasionally

Fill a large saucepan half full with water. Bring to a boil over Low Flames or hot coals. Add the olive oil and the noodles. Cook about 10 minutes or until noodles are tender. Drain the water from the pasta and rinse with cold water.

While the pasta is cooking combine peanut butter, soy sauce, sesame oil and hot chili sauce in a small cook pot and warm slightly until peanut butter melts and mixes well with the other ingredients. Pour this over the noodles when they are done. Top with Chicken and sliced red pepper.

Worth the Effort

Peggy's River Wings
Prepare at Home, Heat at the River

2 pounds Chicken Wing pieces
¼ cup Franks Red Hot® Sauce
¼ cup Valentina's® Mexican Sauce
 2 Tablespoons butter
Large aluminum Foil Pan, Lasagna size
Chunky Blue Cheese Dressing

Cut wing tips off chicken and discard. Cut wings in half at the
joint. Bake in a turkey roaster at 300° for 45 minutes or until
grease is rendered from the wings.   Remove from oven and
and discard the grease.   Transfer ½ of the wings to a foil
lined broiler pan. Low Broil the wings on the middle shelf of
the oven, turning often until browned. Watch closely so they
don't burn. Remove from the oven and place on a cookie
sheet to cool. Repeat with the rest of the wings.

Melt Butter in a quart size glass measuring bowl in the
microwave. Stir in the Franks Red Hot Sauce and the
Valentina's Mexican Sauce. When the wings are cool pack
them into a gallon size self sealing plastic bag. Pour the hot
sauce mix into the bag over the wings and seal tightly.

Refrigerate up to 2 days or freeze.

In Camp: Pour chicken wings into the aluminum foil pan and
heat over medium coals turning often until crispy.
Serve with Blue Cheese Dressing.

Fresh Salsa

8 people ~ tools: cutting board, slicing knife,
tight lidded container

5 firm Roma tomatoes
1 sweet onion
1 lime or 2 tablespoons lime juice
1 tablespoon fresh cilantro or ½ teaspoon cilantro paste
1 teaspoon salt
Optional: 1 jalapeno, seeds discarded, finely chopped

Chop tomato and onion into small pieces and place in lidded dish. Squeeze in sliced lime, add cilantro and salt Refrigerate for at least an hour. Keep refrigerated up to three days.

Hot German Potato Salad

8 people ~ tools: large soup pot, serving spoon, slicing knife, cutting board

10 red potatoes, boiled with skin on
2 pounds Kielbasa cut into bite size pieces
½ pound bacon
2 medium onions diced
2 stalks celery diced
½ cup apple cider vinegar
1 ½ cup mayonnaise
2 teaspoons sugar

Boil potatoes in the soup pot on the grill over low flames until potatoes are slightly firm. Remove from heat and remove potatoes from the water and place on the side of the grill to cool. Discard water. Slice bacon into small pieces and cook in pot until crispy. Drain any grease but leave pan greasy. Slice Kielbasa into bite size pieces and add to pot. Chop onion and celery and stir into pot. Move to the side of the grill and stir in mayonnaise, vinegar and sugar. Cut Potatoes into bite size pieces and gently mix into sauce. Serve hot.

The Big and Easy Pasty

A big meal for 4 people
Bake at home, pack for the mountain, river or road

1 ½ pounds ground round steak
14 ounce can corned beef hash, I prefer Hormel®Home Style
1 medium size onion, finely chopped
4 cups diced frozen potato hash browns
1 ounce package au jus mix
1 teaspoon black pepper
Package of 2 prepared refrigerated pie crust
        I prefer Pillsbury® pie crust
Parchment paper on sheet pan

Thaw the frozen potatoes in a large bowl and press out any moisture with a paper towel. Sprinkle on au jus mix and pepper. Mix in onion. Divide ground round and corned beef in small chunks around the top of the potatoes. Mix well. Divide in half and press tightly together like meatloaf. Cover clean sheet pan with parchment paper. Unroll the dough on parchment paper and place half of the mix on one side of the dough, fold the other half over and seal like a turnover. Use a fork to put tiny holes in the pie dough to vent the steam. Repeat with second pie dough. Bake at 400 degrees for 45 minutes or until golden brown. Cool completely before cutting in half for 4 pies, wrap in alluminum foil, refrigerate up to 4 days or freeze until needed.

In camp, warm in foil over medium hot coals and serve with hot brown gravy. Or eat cold with Ketchup.

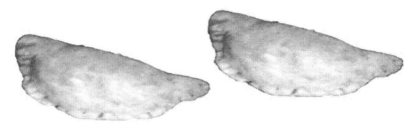

We flew into Schafer Meadows in the Great Bear ~ Bob
Marshall Wilderness with pilot friends for the annual
maintenance work party. Governor Judy Martz flew in for
dinner and personally made Fry Bread for 50 people. For
that crowd however, she used a Propane Fry Cooker.
Nice memory. ~ Thanks, Lorrie and Dave Gates!

Fry Bread
4-6 people~ tools: Fry pan with high sides or large soup pot

3 cups flour
1 teaspoon salt
2 teaspoons baking powder
¾ cup dried milk powder
1 tablespoon sugar
1 cup water
1 cup canola oil

AT HOME: Mix all ingredients except water and oil together in a large seal tight plastic bag.

IN CAMP: Shake out ½ cup dry ingredients onto a plate with sides (a paper plate on a Frisbee works well). Drizzle a little oil around the inside plastic of your flour bag to help keep your dough from sticking. Pour water into the bag containing the flour. Press out the air and seal the bag. Then mix dough by squeezing the bag with your fingers ~ *If dough doesn't mix easily open the bag a little.* Set aside.

Pour canola oil into your fry pan and heat over hot coals until a pinch of dough will bubble in the oil. Scoop a spoonful of dough onto the floured plate, flip then flatten with the back of the spoon. Cut a slit in the center of the dough then transfer to your frypan. Fry both sides and transfer to paper towel.

Sprinkle with sugar for dessert, use for taco shells or
Serve with Green Chili Soup recipe on page 119.

Roast Beast

12 people ~ tools: large serving spoon, leather cook gloves

Cook at Home and Pack
  I cooked this and packed it 7 miles into Grayling Lake in the Pioneer Mountains. My friends were really impressed.

8   pound rump roast
12 medium size Idaho potatoes, cleaned and quartered
2   pound bag of carrots, cleaned, sliced into 2 inch pieces
2   large onions
1   package Lipton® dry onion soup mix
2   packages brown gravy mix
3   cups water
canola oil
2 disposable aluminum lasagna pans with foil lid
Optional: 2 loaves garlic bread packaged in foil

At Home:
Cover the bottom of a large crock pot with oil. Put the vegetables in the bottom of the pot and the roast on top of the vegetables. Mix gravy and soup mix with water and pour over the top of the roast. Slow cook for 8 to 10 hours until meat is tender. *(or in the oven at 325 degrees for 4 hours)*

Slice beef and layer with vegetables in lasagna pans. Pour gravy into zip lock bag and seal (if you don't have at least 3 cups of gravy supplement with a can of gravy. Place bag of gravy on top of beef and vegetables. Seal with foil lid. Freeze overnight. Wrap in a kitchen size garbage bag and seal with tape. *This is a good second or third night meal as it may take awhile to thaw.*

In Camp:
Prepare a bed of hot coals. Remove gravy from the pan and pour over meat and vegetables. Cover with foil lid and reheat on grill over hot coals turning occasionally to heat evenly. This could take about an hour so don't wait until dark. It doesn't take much watching and there is no cleanup.

Wildflower Pit Turkey

10 people ~ tools: shovel, heat resistant gloves, heavy duty aluminum foil ~ extra wide, white rope and stakes

12 to 15 pound turkey, thawed, cleaned, insides removed
Canola oil, salt and seasoning.

Dig a square pit about 3 feet wide, long and deep. Collect baseball size rocks (not river rock as they can explode). Build a large breakfast campfire over the rocks and enjoy your breakfast. When fire has died down shovel half the hot rocks and coals into the bottom of the pit. Wrap your turkey in 4 to 5 separate layers of foil, changing directions of foil with each layer. Place turkey into the pit and shovel remaining rocks and coals around the sides of the turkey. Bury with extracted dirt. Rope off your area for safety.

Go and play, enjoy your day. Turkey will be done in 4 or 5 hours but it won't hurt to leave it longer. Dig it up carefully so as not to puncture your foil and "Dirt the Bird"

RMRTFE Rocky Mountain Rough Terrain Frisbee experts

A Montana campfire book would not be complete without mention of the elusive WILDFLOWER. An annual invitation only frisbee event dating back to 1976. The location has always been a highly guarded secret.

Desserts and Finishers

Cinnamon Roll Sundae
Per Person

5 inch aluminum foil pie pan
Bakery Cinnamon Roll
1 teaspoon regular margarine ~ not whipped not light
Vanilla Ice Cream
Caramel Topping
Chopped walnuts

Spread margarine in the bottom of pie pan and up the edges. Put cinnamon roll on top of margarine and place on grill over low coals until cinnamon roll is warmed. Watch closely so it doesn't burn. Top with ice cream, caramel and walnuts.

Toasted Donuts
Per Person

One or two glazed donuts per person
Frosted donuts do not work however fruit filled donuts do.
Place on grill over low coals.
Flip once to lightly brown both sides.

204

Fried Apple Pie

6 people ~ Tools: Tall soup pot, slotted spoon

13 ounce package puff pastry sheet
4 crisp apples
4 Tablespoons Lemon juice
Canola oil
10 ounce container prepared cream cheese frosting

Peel and slice apples into small pieces. Drizzle with lemon juice to coat all of the apple pieces. *This is to keep the apples from turning brown and gives them a nice flavor.*

Roll out the puff pastry onto parchment paper to keep it from sticking to any surface. Cut into 6 squares, reserving one very small slice. Remove the apples from the lemon juice with the slotted spoon and drain onto a paper towel. Fill half of each square of pastry with apples and fold over into a triange. Seal the edges.

Pour about two inches of oil into the pan and heat on grill over hot coals or low flame for about a minute. When you think the oil might be hot enough to fry your pies, drop a piece of the reserved dough into the oil. The dough should brown slowly ~ if the oil is too hot, move your pan to the side of the grill to cool a little.

Drop your pies one or two at a time into the hot oil. Turn once using the slotted spoon. Remove to paper towel and spread on frosting while pie is still warm to create a glaze.

Fried Cinnamon Sticks

13 ounce package puff pastry sheet
2 cups brown sugar
2 tablespoons ground cinnamon

Mix together the brown sugar and cinnamon on a sheet pan.Slice pastry into 2x6 inch pieces. Twist without crushing the dough. Fry using the directions for the pie above. Roll in brown sugar and cinnamon while hot.

Chocolate Chip Skillet Cookie

Tools: cast iron skillet, mixing pan, parchment paper, Gallon size seal tight plastic bag, alluminum foil

spray oil
2   cups all-purpose flour
½   teaspoon baking soda
1½ cups butter
¼   cup sugar
½   cup dark brown sugar packed
1   teaspoon maple extract
2   eggs
1   cup chocolate chips
½   cup walnut pieces

Coat a 10 to 12 inch cast iron skillet with non stick spray. Cut a piece of parchment paper to fit into the bottom of the skillet and up the sides about an inch. Press into the skillet.

Soften butter in the sun or on a peice of alluminum foil on a rock near the grill.

Combine flour and baking soda into the seal tight bag and shake well to mix, add sugar and shake again. Crack eggs and drop them into the flour mix, add softened butter and maple extract. Squeeze the air from the bag and seal. Squ sh together until the dough is well mixed. Add chocolate chips and walnuts and mix again.

Press into the skillet and place on the grill over medium low coals. Cover skillet with alluminum foil and cook for 12 to 15 minutes. If the bottom appears to be browning too quickly, move the pan to the side of the grill to cool it down.

Serve with ice cream if you have it.

Crispy Apple Flautas

6 people ~ tools: fry pan, spatula, aluminum foil

4 apples peeled and sliced
2 teaspoon lemon juice
2 tablespoons butter
3 tablespoons sugar
½ teaspoon cinnamon
¼ cup water

6 flour tortillas
6 pieces of alluminum foil, tortilla sized
3 tablespoons margarine

Put peeled and sliced apples in the fry pan. Drizzle with lemon juice to coat. Dot with butter. Sprinkle with sugar and cinnamon. Place fry pan on grill over medium hot coals. Add just enough water to keep the apples from burning.

Spread both sides of each tortilla with softened margarine. Sprinkle both sides with sugar and cinnamon. Place each tortilla onto a piece of alluminum foil on the grill and cook until lightly crisp, on both sides. Fold in half and fill with hot apple mix.

Caramelized Pineapple Skewers

6 people ~ tools: wooden skewers, large sharp knife

1 pineapple
2 cups brown sugar

Soak skewers in water
Slice Pineapple lengthwise and
 trim off the exterior and core.
Thread onto skewers
Roll in brown sugar
Place on grill over hot coals
Turn occasionally

Easier Apple Flautas
4 people ~ aluminum foil, can opener

4 Flour Tortillas
1 can apple pie filling
sugar
cinnamon
softened margarine

Spread both sides of each tortilla with margarine and sprinkle with sugar and cinnamon. Spread one side with apple pie filling and roll up. Wrap in foil and place on grill over hot coals. Cook until hot and crispy, turning from time to time to keep from burning.

Easy Cherry Cheesecake

24 ounce tub of ready to eat cheesecake filling
21 ounce can cherry pie filling
Package of 12 ice cream sugar cones

Layer cheesecake and pie filling in ice cream cones. Pie crust also works but the cones are more fun.

Campfire Berries and Cake
6 – 8 people ~ tools: 8x12 aluminum foil pan, spatula

1 angel food cake
8 ounce package frozen fruit Triple Berry Blend
            (blueberry, raspberry, strawberry)
1 quart fresh raspberries
marshmallow cream
butter flavored spray cooking oil

Spray foil pan with cooking oil. Slice cake in thick slabs and arrange in the pan. Place on grill over medium hot coals. Toast one side and flip. Remove from heat. Arrange berries around the cake and dot with marshmallow cream. Return to grill and heat until the fruit is hot and marshmallow melty.

Dirt Cake
8 people ~ tools: 8x12 aluminum foil pan, spatula,
*   mixing bowl and spoon*

1   package Oreo Cookies ~ 20 ounces
2   packages cream cheese ~ 16 ounces
16 ounces cool whip, thawed
2 chocolate snack pack pudding cups

Mix softened cream cheese, powdered sugar and thawed cool whip together. Stir in pudding.

Pour cookies into the foil pan and smash with spatula until crumbly. Stir in cream cheese & cool whip mix. Put in cooler for ½ hour or until cookies are softened.

Huckleberry Crepes

6 - 12 people ~ 6 inch non- stick fry pan, spatula,
Medium size metal bowl, rotary hand beater

Simple Crepes   *about 12 crepes*
I make crepes at home and layer in parchment paper.
Store in Seal Tight plastic bags. May be frozen for 1 months

3 eggs
1 ¼ cup milk
1 ½ cup all-purpose flour
2 tablespoons melted butter, or margarine.
2 teaspoons sugar
Butter flavored cooking spray oil
Parchment paper

Whisk together eggs and milk. Add butter and sugar. Stir in flour. Whisk or stir until creamy smooth.

Spray fry pan with oil and heat over medium hot coals. Pour about ¼ cup crepe batter into pan and quickly tilt the pan in all directions so batter covers the pan in a thin layer. Cook about one minute. Crepe is ready for flipping when it slides easily in the pan. Flip crepe and cook another 30 seconds. Sprinkle with a little more sugar. Stack between layers of parchment paper to prevent them from sticking together.

Filling

1 12 ounce jar Huckleberry Jam
12 ounces frozen Huckleberries (or blueberries) thawed
16 ounces Heavy Whipping Cream
2 tsp sugar

Pour whipping cream and sugar into a cold metal bowl. Pass around to let everyone take a turn whipping the cream. Spread each crepe with Jam and 3 tablespoons berries. Roll up. Top with berry juice and whipped cream.

HAPPY HOUR

August In Dearborn River, Montana

Sunshine Tea
8 black tea bags
½ cup honey
Juice of 3 lemons
2 cups vodka or gin
1 lemon sliced

Fill a 2 quart glass jar half full with water. Put in tea bags and place in the sun to steep for about an hour. Discard tea bags. Stir in honey, lemon juice and vodka. Add ice cubes to fill jar. Serve in tall glasses filled with ice cubes. Top with lemon slice.

Sunday Morning Ceasar
2 ounces gin or vodka
Clamato Juice
Tall glass
Stalk of celery
1 Tbsp Worcestershire sauce or to taste
Lemon pepper

Saint Regis Mary Mix
3 tall drinks

Juice of one lemon
3 ½ cups tomato juice
3 Tbsp Worcestershire sauce
3 dashes Tobasco
1 tsp freshly ground black pepper
1 tsp cayenne pepper
1 tsp celery salt
1 tsp whole

Pour ingredients into a container and shake well. Use immediately or refrigerate. To prepare one drink, fill glass with ice and add 2 oz vodka or gin. Fill with Mary Mix.

Shoot the Rapids
Tools: insulated travel cup

1 can or bottle of light lager beer
2 fingers good tequila, 100% Agave
ice cubes
slice of lime

Ruby River
1 cup Ruby Red Grapefruit Juice
½ cup London Dry Gin
½ cup tonic water.
Poured over ice and stirred.

Old Faithful Old Fashioned
2 ounces bourbon

1 dash bitters
Club soda
Orange slice
Ice Cubes

Manhattan 406
2 shots rye whiskey
1 shot sweet vermouth
1 dash bitters
Orange twist and maraschino cherry on a toothpick
Ice Cubes

The Horse Shoe
Ice Cubes in a high ball glass…. No plastic
3 fingers Elijah Craig 12 year old
Sparkling water
squeeze of lemon

Fire Fly
2 ounces Jack Daniels
½ cup unsweetened ruby red grapefruit juice
Sparkling water
Ice

Rattlesnake
3 fingers Good American Bourbon
Real ice Cubes, not bag ice
rattlesnake venom if you have some

"Too much of anything is bad,
but too much good whiskey is barely enough."   Mark Twain

Prickly Pear
2 ounces silver tequila,
1/3 cup Pomegranate Juice,
2/3 cup ruby red grapefruit juice
Ginger Ale

Stillwater Sunset
¼ cup unsweetened orange juice
¼ cup unsweetened cranberry juice
¼ cup vodka
Tall glass
Ice   Shaken, not stirred ; }

Bee Sting
2 shots vodka
½ shot frozen lemonade
Crushed ice
Topped with maraschino cherry and slice of lemon

Cemetery Island
2 shots Silver Tequila
1 shot vodka
1 shot of Blueberry Juice, unsweetened
Sparkling Water
Crushed Ice in a tall glass

Swingin Bridge
1 ounce gin
1 ounce rum
1 ounce tequila
1 ounce triple sec
 tall glass
Ice cubes
Top with coca cola

Kootenai River

Highland Martini
½ cup Bombay Gin
Rocks glass and ice
Green olives optional

The distinct flavor of gin comes from juniper berries.
Montana grows a lot of juniper and I have often thought it
might be fun to try making some. Juniper berries are also a
natural stimulant.   Late to bed, and late to rise : }

Rocky Mountain Summer
2 ounces New Amsterdam Gin ~ hints of orange & lemon
2 orange slices
Tall lemonade glass
Ice

Fill glass with ice. Add gin and fill glass with water. Squeeze
one slice of orange into the glass and garnish with another
orange slice.

Margarita
1 1/2 ounces tequila (100 percent agave)
1 ounce Cointreau
1 lime freshly squeezed
Margarita Salt
1 thin lime wedge, crushed Ice

Copper Mule	**Grapefruit Mule**
2 ounces vodka	1 ½ ounces vodka
½ ounce fresh lime juice	¼ freshly squeezed grapefruit
3 ounces ginger beer	4 ounces ginger beer
Lime wedge, for garnish	Grapefruit wedge for garnish

A Copper Mug is essential to a proper Mule. The insulating
properties of the metal makes the ginger beer icy cold and
boosts the fizziness of the beer. You can buy a copper mug
in many liquor stores and gift shops, but if you are passing
through Butte, consider buying yours in the Copper City.

"I drink my champagne when I'm happy
And when I'm sad.
Sometimes I drink it when I'm alone.
When I have company, I consider it obligatory.
I trifle with it if I'm not hungry
and drink it when I am.
Otherwise I never touch it ~ unless I'm thirsty"

Lily Bollinger ~ London Daily Mail, October 17, 1961

Champeggy

1 bottle champagne BRUT as good as your budget allows
1 bottle Cointreau, or orange liqueur, or orange juice

Freeze Champagne to slushy. Pack in Icy part of cooler.
Pour generously. Season to taste with orange liqueur.

Champagne Cocktails
1 bottle champagne BRUT as good as your budget allows

Champagne, Brandy and Maraschino Cherry

Champagne, Cranberry Juice, Cranberries

Champagne, Pear Brandy, Orange Slice

Champagne, Tequila, Limes, Plenty of Ice

Champagne, Peach Schnapps, sliced peaches

Lake of the Clouds
2 ounces vodka
1 ounce white crème de cacao
1 ounce half and half
Crushed ice

216

Hot Buttered Rum
Per person

1 ½ teaspoons butter, softened
1 tablespoon brown sugar
1 teaspoon powdered sugar
Pinch of ground cinnamon
1 jigger dark Jamaican rum
1 cup boiling water
1 jigger orphan girl cream
Dash of nutmeg

Combine butter, brown sugar and powdered sugar in a tall coffee cup. Stir the mix together with a fork. Pour in the rum and fill the cup with boiling water. Stir until butter is melted. Top with Orphan Girl, and sprinkle with a dash of nutmeg.

After Midnight
½ cup Strong Black Coffee
2 ounces Kalua
1 ounce Orphan Girl or Baileys

It was a dark and Jameson quiet morning,
empty whiskey bottle on the table.

"5:17 a.m. I woke – could not go back to sleep.

Almost quiet, my furtive steps did not rouse the late night revelers.
I took the coffee outside.
I wanted the fresh beans and spilled too much in the wet sand.

Joy, no one woke as the grinder worked the beans.

CAMPING WITH KIDS

The Highland Mountains, Montana

The Don't Forget About … List

Water Bottle, Water, Water, More Water
Lifejackets, Swimsuit, Towel
Sunscreen, Insect Repellent, Bandaids
Band -Aid® Hurt Free Antiseptic Pain Relieving Liquid

Shorts and T-shirts, Sun Hat
Water Shoes, Tennis Shoes,
Socks
Sweatpants, Long Sleeve Tops
Warm Fleece Jacket, Warm Hat
Wash Cloth, Soap, Lotion
Toothbrush
Grocery bags for wet and dirty
clothes

Nap blanket
Sleeping Bag and pad, Pillow
Pajamas
Flashlights for kids

Camp Chair, Baby Swing Chair
Toilet Paper, Paper Towels,
Diapers for babies
Tarp for Toys or Rain Cover
Bright Colored Rope to rope off danger zones
            Or for Rain Tarp

Water Bottle, Hot Cocoa Mix
Instant Oatmeal, Juice Boxes
Peanut butter, Hot Dogs
Marshmallows, roasting sticks

Easy Kids Menus and Recipes

Kids need to eat in the morning.

Breakfast at 11 is fine with me but kids need to eat in the morning. Sometimes a spoon full of peanut butter is enough but a spoon full of peanut butter in instant oatmeal is better. Fix it when your coffee water is hot, not boiling, and before you add coffee to the pot ; }

Ice Cream Cone Breakfast Cups

Flat bottom ice cream cone
Vanilla yogurt
Top with fruity pebbles

Hot Bites

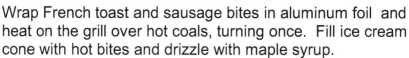

Flat bottom ice cream cone
Frozen packaged French toast bites
Frozen fully cooked sausage bites
Optional: maple syrup

Wrap French toast and sausage bites in aluminum foil and heat on the grill over hot coals, turning once. Fill ice cream cone with hot bites and drizzle with maple syrup.

PB Jamwhich

2 Frozen Homestyle Waffles
Peanut Butter and Jelly
½ banana sliced

Put together like a sandwich and cut in half. Wrap in aluminum foil. Heat on grill over hot coals, turning once.

Donut Kabobs

Mini Glazed Donuts
Fresh Strawberries
      Optional: Chocolate Ice Cream Sauce

Thread donuts and strawberries on a clean and sharpened willow stick like a kabob. Warm over medium hot coals. This won't take long. Drizzle chocolate Ice cream sauce over strawberries before eating.

Nutella French Toast
6 people ~ tools: aluminum foil

12 ounce package Frozen French Toast Sticks
13 ounce jar Hazelnut Spread

Wrap French Toast Sticks in aluminum foil and place on the grill over hot coals. Heat about 10 minutes, turning often.

Dip in Hazelnut Spread

Easiest Pancakes

4 to 6 people/12 pancakes ~ tools: fry pan or griddle, spatula, mixing bowl, large serving spoon

2 cups Complete Buttermilk Pancake Mix
1 1/3 cups water
Canola oil
Toppings: Butter, syrup, peanut butter, fruit topping

Combine pancake mix and water in a bowl and stir well. Heat griddle on grill over medium hot coals. Coat the bottom of the pan with oil. Spoon pancake mix onto the griddle. Flip when top of the cake gets little bubbles and the bottom appears firm.

May I Bring the Wagon? Please?

I can help unpack the truck and haul around the baby.
I can sleep at the campfire and you can pull me to the tent.
And, it's a good place for crawdads and rocks.

Simply Mac and Cheese

4 people ~ tools: Medium size saucepan, 8x8 aluminum foil cake pan, serving spoon, cook gloves

8 ounce pkg large elbow macaroni
4 cups water
2 tablespoons canola oil
1 cup shredded Mild Cheddar Cheese
2 tablespoon Parmesan
½ cup milk
4 tablespoons butter
Salt and pepper to taste

Pour water into saucepan to boil on grill over hot coals. Add oil and macaroni to boiling water and stir once. Continue to cook until pasta is tender. Remove from heat and drain any remaining water.

Melt butter in foil pan on grill over medium hot coals. Pour in milk and cooked macaroni. Evenly distribute cheeses over the top and gently stir into pasta. Move pan to the side of the grill to heat through without burning. *If macaroni seems too watery add a little more parmesan cheese.*

Pizza Mac and Cheese

4 people ~ tools: can opener, 8x8 aluminum foil cake pan

8 ounce pkg small elbow macaroni
15 ounce can of Pizza Sauce.
2 cups shredded Mozzarella cheese
4 ounce can sliced black olives
Pepperoni slices

Use recipe above to cook macaroni. Drain water from cooked pasta and pour into a foil cake pan. Top with cheese, pepperoni and olives. Cover and place on grill over medium or low coals for cheese to melt.

Gooey Cheese Loaf
4 people ~ tools: Aluminum foil

1 loaf French bread
½ cup butter (1 stick)
10 slices American cheese
Optional: spaghetti sauce, pepperoni, black olives,

Cut the bread into one inch slices almost to the bottom of the loaf but not all the way through ~ about 10 slices. Butter one side of each slice of bread. Cut cheese in halves and place between the bread slices.

Wrap bread in aluminum foil, twisting the ends of the foil to make handles for turning. Heat on the grill 4 inches from hot coals for about 10 minutes, turning once.

Lil Buddy Kabobs
4 people ~ tools: wooden skewers, can opener

16 ounce package Cocktail size wieners
16 ounce package Frozen Meatballs
2 14 ounce cans whole New Potatoes
4 Large Dill Pickles cut in kabob size chunks
15 ounce can of Nacho Cheese Sauce

Open the can of cheese sauce, set on the edge of the grill to warm slowwwly. Stir once or twice.
Soak the skewers in water for 15 minutes. Alternate wieners, potatoes, meatballs, and pickles on the skewers. Grill over medium hot coals until browned and hot. Dip in cheese.

Walking Tacos
4 people ~ tools: high sided fry pan, serving spoon, forks

2 pounds lean ground beef
1 ounce package taco seasoning
1 cup water
12 one ounce packages nacho cheese chips
16 ounce package shredded Mexican Blend Cheese
2 Tablespoons canola oil

Warm oil in fry pan on grill over hot coals. Crumble ground beef into hot oil and cook until meat is no longer pink. Stir often.

Drain grease from cooked meat and wipe pan with paper towel. Pour in water and taco seasoning. Return to medium hot coals and cook until sauce bubbles and thickens. Remove from heat.

Open one bag at a time and spoon in taco meat. Top with cheese. Eat from the bag with a spoon.

Walking Salad
Per person ~ tools: knife, paper plate, toothpicks

Sliced Bologna
Sliced Cheese
Lettuce Leaf
Mustard or Mayonnaise

Spread bologna with mustard or mayonnaise. Roll bologna around the cheese and wrap with a lettuce leaf. Secure with a toothpick but remove toothpick before handing to small children.

Peanut Butter Apple Snack

Per person ~ tools: sharp knife, paper plate

1 apple
2 tablespoons peanut butter

Slice apple in 4 pieces. Slice out the apple core. Slice each piece again so you have 8 apple slices. Spread with peanut butter.

Snack Platter

3 or more persons ~ tools: sharp knife, paper plate

Apple slices
Celery Sticks
Cauliflower Bites
Broccoli Bites
15 ounce jar of nacho cheese dip or ranch dressing dip

Watermelon Squared

3 - 6 or more persons depending on size of watermelon
tools: sharp knife, paper plate

1 seedless watermelon

Cut in thick slices. Cut each slice in 4 pieces leaving on the rind. Place on grill over medium hot coals, flip once.

As the water evaporates the melon develops a caramelized exterior and a flavorful juicy center.

Easy Burrito's
4 people ~ tools: can opener, spoon,
4 squares aluminum foil

1 16 ounce can Rosarita® no fat traditional refried beans
4 Flour Tortillas
8 ounces shredded Mexican Blend Cheese
Spray Canola Oil
Mild red taco sauce
Optional Fillings: Cooked rice, chopped tomatoes,

Place one tortilla on each square of foil. Spray tortilla with canola oil. Flip over and spread refried beans on each tortilla. Distribute cheese evenly on top of beans. Fold burrito style. Wrap foil around each burrito. Heat on grill over medium hot coals for about 10 minutes. Turn often to prevent burning. Serve with mild taco sauce.

Quesadillas
4 people ~ tools: 8 squares alluminum foil, can opener
You can make these at home and store in a seal tight bag

8 soft corn tortilla's
12 ounces shredded Mexican blend cheese
Spray canola oil

Optional: 1 can sliced black olives,
2 Roma tomato's chopped

Place each tortilla on one square of foil. Spray with oil and flip so oiled side is on the foil. Top tortillas with cheese and other ingredients. Fold in half. Wrap foil around the filled tortilla. Place on grill over medium hot coals for about 5 minutes, flip and warm the other side.

Pizza Potato

4 people ~ tools: non-stick aluminum foil, slicing knife, can opener, spoons, cooks gloves

4 potatoes, previously baked
15 ounce can Pizza Sauce
8 ounce pkg shredded Pizza Cheese
3 ounce pkg sliced Pepperoni
2 ½ ounce can sliced Black Olives

Set can of pizza sauce in a warm place for ½ hour but not on the grill unless you open the can first. Cut each potato in half lengthwise and wrap in foil. Place on grill to heat, rolling occasionally so as not to burn. Open center of hot baked potato and fluff insides. Stir pizza sauce in the can and spoon into potatoes. Top with cheese, pepperoni and olives.

Chili Cheese Potato's

2 people ~ tools: Sheet pan, spatula, slicing knife, gloves

2 previously baked potatoes cut in half
15 ounce can Chili Con Carne with Beans
8 ounces Shredded Cheddar Cheese
8 ounce tub Sour Cream

Cut each potato half way through and wrap in foil. Place on grill to heat, rolling occasionally so as not to burn. Heat chili in a sauce pan over medium hot coals, stirring frequently. Open center of hot baked potato and fluff insides. Spoon in chili. Top with cheese and sour cream.

Potato Nacho's

2 people ~ tools: aluminum foil, gloves, spray cooking oil

2 previously baked potatoes
1 can nacho cheese sauce

Slice potatoes onto foil, spray with cooking oil, wrap and place on grill over hot coals until crispy. Cover with cheese

Grilled Cheese
1 person ~tools: aluminum foil

2 slices bread
2 slices medium cheddar cheese
1 tablespoon softened butter
Butter flavored cooking spray oil

Spray aluminum foil with cooking oil. Spread both sides of bread with butter.   Sandwich the cheese and wrap in foil. Place on Grill over medium coals and toast. Turning often.

Bob's Surprise
Make a Peanut Butter and Jelly Sandwich with a slice of medium cheddar cheese and Grill it in aluminum foil as above. *SURPRISE, it's really good!*

Root Beer Beans
8 people ~ tools: deep fry pan, can opener, paper bowls

8 slices bacon
2 cans pinto beans
2 cans cannellini beans
1 cup root beer (not diet)
1/2 cup ketchup
1/4 cup dark brown sugar

Cook bacon in fry pan over medium hot coals until crispy. Remove from pan to a paper towel. Wipe the bacon grease from the pan with a paper towel. Open the beans and drain the liquid then add the beans to the pan along with the root beer, ketchup and brown sugar. Stir well and return to medium coals. Allow to simmer until liquid is reduced. Crumble the cooked bacon over the beans before serving.

Big Foot Chili Dogs

6 people ~ tools: saucepan, can opener, serving spoon, paper plates

6 foot long hot dogs
16 ounce can chili with beans
6 foot long hot dog buns
12 ounce bag shredded cheddar cheese

Open Chili and pour into saucepan. Place on grill over medium hot coals. Stir occasionally to keep from burning. Make 3 or 4 thin diagonal cuts in each of the hot dogs. Place on the grill over hot coals. Turn as necessary to grill without burning.

Assemble the Big Foot. Place hot dog on the bun, top with chili and cheese.

Shrimp Baskets

4 person ~tools: aluminum foil

2 pounds EZ peel shrimp, extra large
4 pieces frozen corn on the cob
Margarine, *not water added margarine*
Lemon Pepper

Cut corn into 3 inch pieces. Sprinkle Shrimp with lemon pepper and divide corn and shrimp onto 4 squares of aluminum foil. Season and dot with margarine. Wrap up tightly and place on grill over medium hot coals. Turn occasionally. Should be hot in about 30 minutes.
Open like a basket.

Snicker More

per person ~ tools: stainless steel skewer with handle or green willow, cooking end shaved thin

Campfire Marshmallows
Mini Snickers®
Snickers should be fresh and soft. If they break up when putting them on the stick, warm in your hand for a minute.

Press 1 mini snickers between 2 marshmallows, sealing edges. Skewer and roast over NO FLAME coals. Turn constantly until mallow is golden brown, not burned.

Milky Way

4 to 8 people ~ tools: aluminum foil pie pan

8 Oreo® Cookie's
8 mini Milky Way® bars

Sandwich one Milky Way between each Oreo cookie. Place in pie pan and warm on grill over medium low coals until milky way is melty, turning once.

Big Dipper

per person

Ice Cream Cone
Vanilla Yogurt
Frozen Raspberries

This one is easy. Layer yogurt, raspberries, yogurt, raspberries. Yummy, fruity, healthy dessert

Cherry Pie Cones
4 - 6 people ~ spoons, can opener

Flat bottom Ice cream cone cups
1 can 21 ounce cherry pie filling
4 pack snack size vanilla puddings
Optional: Reddi-whip® whipped dairy cream

Spoon vanilla pudding into ice cream cones. Top with Cherry Pie Filling. Spray with whipping cream.

Oreo Pie
4 - people ~ spoons

4 3 ounce vanilla pudding cups
2 3.5 ounce package Chocolate Oreo® Mini Go Cups
4 aluminum foil tart shell pans

Crumble Oreos into tart shells. Top with vanilla pudding and a maraschino cherry.

Frosted Pretzels
1 carton prepared vanilla or chocolate frosting
1 bag pretzel sticks to dip in the frosting

Strawberry Fluff
Place a fresh strawberry on a roasting stick or skewer. Dip in Marshmallow cream. Roast over coals until marshmallow is lightly browned. (*usually less than a minute*)

A Better Krispy

Cook at home and pack for camp

½ pound butter
16 ounce bag mini marshmallows
12 cups fruity pebbles cereal

Cover sheet pan with parchment paper. Melt butter in a large soup pot. Stir marshmallows into the butter and heat until marshmallows are completely melted. Stir in fruity pebbles. Pour onto parchment paper and roll into two long logs using the edges of the paper.   Leave the paper on the krispies and cool completely. Cut logs in half so they fit into a gallon size seal tight plastic bag.

Banana Split

Banana
Chocolate chips
Mini marshmallows

Slice a wedge out of the center of a banana without removing the peel. Fill with marshmallows and chocolate. Close the open peel. Wrap in aluminum foil and place on the grill over hot coals, about 10 minutes.

Healthier split ~ substitute the chocolate for sliced strawberries and use only enough marshmallows to bind the fruit together.

CAMPFIRE STORIES

Windigo
by Peggy Racicot

It was a clear quiet night, warm for mid September. The stars twinkled like diamonds where we camped high above the valley of the Sun River. We sat by the fire until midnight before climbing into our tents.

I was nearly asleep when the wind tore through the trees with a fierceness I had not heard before. A tree near our tent cracked as the top half was sheared off and fell hard. My two brothers in the tent next to ours screamed. I tried to see but the wind had flattened the poles of our tent to the ground and the fabric billowed close to my face. It was hard to breath. Dad struggled with the zipper to open the door. As soon as the door was open the wind entered and the tent filled up like a balloon. He got out of the tent to see about the boys who were still screaming for help. Through the opening I could see their tent moving. The wind was under their rain fly and lifting their tent like a kite ~ with them in it. They had not staked down their tent and it was perilously close to flying over the edge of the cliff where the Sun River raged 30 feet below.

Dad caught the boy's tent and struggled to pull it back. The moment they emerged from the tent it sailed away like a kite to join the stars.

A thick snow laden fog descended upon us and the night became deathly still. None of us could sleep so we added wood to the dying embers of the fire and huddled around the campfire until the darkness finally gave up to dawn.

Dad was cooking breakfast when a thin ragged man emerged from the fog. Grey teeth grinned through thin lips and hollow cheeks. Patches of his skull showed through dirty long grey hair. When he stepped into our campfire circle I could see thin blue veins through skin that protruded from the worn out fabric of his ragged clothes.

But he spoke in a soft and gentle voice to my father, "I smelled your breakfast. Would you have anything to spare? I have been traveling across the Rockies and through the Glaciers of Canada. My journey will end soon."

My father nodded and he sat when dad handed him a plate piled high and steaming with hot fried trout, bacon and potatoes. Only then did I notice under the torn ragged edges of his jeans his feet were bare and he sat so closely to the fire that his feet were nearly in the flames.

"I have heard tales of travelers like you." My father said. "Unlikely stories, of men who travel with the wind. Of men crossing an open field and simply vanishing. The Indian legends call them Windigo."

He replied, "For your kindness I will offer you my story, if it will not frighten the children?"

Dad handed him a cup of coffee topped with whiskey and cream. After a long sigh of pleasure, he continued.

"There are others like me, some as young as this child." And when he looked at me with eyes glowing red in the campfire light a fear crept into my soul that I have not yet forgotten.

"I used to live not far from here and I would often come here to fish. One day I was crossing the meadow when a whirlwind of snow and icey fog barrelled through the meadow sweeping me off my feet and far beyond where I could touch the earth and the last sunflower in the grass.

I felt a soaring wave of air beneath me as I was carried higher into the clouds beyond any control of my own body. The meadow disappeared beneath me, the river too.

The wind tore at my clothes and skin as it carried me at a furious speed through the mountain passes and over the glaciers. Ice formed on my skin and I could barely breath.

Then as suddenly as the wind tore me from the earth, it stopped! I tumbled without a parachute for a thousand feet but just before I hit the ground the wind swept under me again to lift me up, softly this time and set me down gently in the wild lands of the northern Rockies.

The wind has taken my soul and I cannot long be gone from its fierce power. In the first years I tried to escape, believing that I might go home again, but always a fever would come upon me. The heat is unbearable. My hands and feet will glow red from the internal fire that consumes me. My only escape from the fever is the cold north wind.

Now I ride the waves of the wind through the clouds, over the mountains, and into the Northern Lights. I come here often because it is close to home and my last memories before I was taken.

I am tired now and no longer feel the excitement of soaring high above the earth, the rush of wind in my face. I only feel cold and hungry and lonely. I want it to end but I am afraid. When the wind lets me go I am afraid of the falling. Will I die from the fall or will I feel the crevasse of a glacier close in around me? To be forever frozen and alone."

Abruptly he stood and looking at my father said " I should go. Thank you for your kindness. You should go too. When I am gone the wind will be taking another."

Then he walked into the fog and disapeared like a snow ghost among the trees. Ten minutes passed and the wind returned with a vengence. It roared through the trees and howled like a banshee. Above it all I heard his voice cry, "NO! Let me rest. Don't take me!"

As suddenly as it began the wind stopped and silence descended on freshly fallen snow. Fifty yards from camp we could clearly see the heel and toe marks of bare feet where his footprints had melted through an inch of snow and burned the grass. The tracks got further and further apart. Then stretched to five and ten feet apart before disappearing.

I heard my dad whisper, " Good luck in your journey".

Underwater Ghost Town
by Peggy Racicot

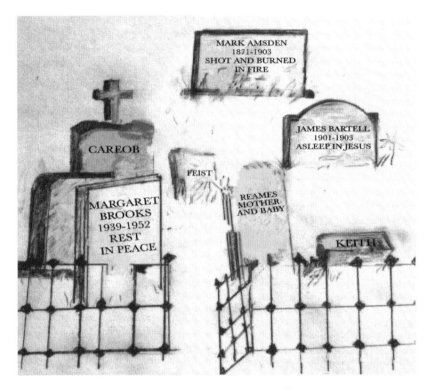

"Hi, my name is Margaret Brookes and I am really a nice person. I live in Canton, Montana. My family was moving to Townsend because Canton was going to be under Canyon Ferry lake. The government made everyone move because of the dam they were building.

Everyone left on my birthday. I was thirteen and my birthday present was a baby kitten. She was white with two black feet and pretty blue eyes. Mom said we would have cake in our new house in Townsend. I was going to ride with my friend Jenny's family because our car had too much stuff in it. Just as everyone was leaving my new kitten got away. She crawled under the cellar door and I went in after her.

239

The door slammed shut and would not open with the water rising against it. No one missed me, or if they did no one found me."

"I was terrified and screamed for help as the cold water rose above my waist. When my face floated to the top of the cellar door my skin turned kind of white and I wasn't cold anymore."

"The door still wouldn't open but I was able to get out of the cellar and into the house. It didn't matter that there was no food because I wasn't hungry."

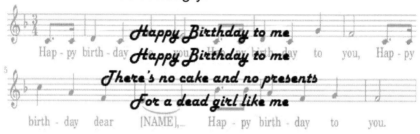

Happy Birthday to me
Happy Birthday to me
There's no cake and no presents
For a dead girl like me

"For a while I saw floaters. Dogs and cats and once a cow. It banged against the side of the house in a scary way. Once I saw a truck sink under the ice. A man got out the window and swam to the surface but couldn't find a way out of the ice. Later he floated by. His hair and beard were all icicles. I was glad to be inside my house because he stared at me through the window. His eyes looked like the white marbles my brother has.

I'm not afraid anymore but I'm really lonely.

Tick tock its six o'clock
Nowhere to go, No one to see
No cookies to bake
In this old house under the lake

Today I saw three girls swimming above me. They are wearing a mask with a tube so they can breathe in the water. I would like one of those. The water is so clear, and the sun is so bright it must be June or July. They look so pretty and I want to swim with them. I run upstairs and open the window to wave. I think they see me because they are coming closer. The one in front with the long blonde hair looks a little like me. Maybe she is my sister.

Oh no! They are swimming away now. I wish she would stay and talk to me! I think I will catch her. If I put her in the cellar no one will find her and I will have a friend forever!

~ ~ ~

WE are sitting on the porch today when a paddle board glides by over our house. We can't see who is there because the paddle is making the water move. It is always interesting to see people because on most days all we see are the fish swimming by.

Oh! It's a girl who looks about our age. She is leaning over the board now looking into the water. Let's wave to her. I don't think she sees us. Let's run upstairs and wave out the window. She is coming closer. I think she sees us!
This is so exciting!

~ ~ ~

There are three girls sitting on the porch now.

"Hello, my name is Margaret Brookes and this is Sara. We have a big house with four bedrooms upstairs. You can see the beach from your bedroom window.

~ ~ ~

I was so excited to have another friend, but we always talk about the same things. I am thinking it would be nice to have a boy in the house. They talk about sports and they are more active. Boys like to fish.

Let's see if we can catch one.

CAMPFIRE MUSIC

We play harmonica, rocks, strings and drums

Pull up a chair and join in the fun.

The Campfire Song
By Ben Racicot

Sittin' around the campfire is one of my favorite places
Everything is easy. Smiles on all the faces.
Flicker of the firelight
There's a billion stars in the sky tonight
Smoke whispers on the rise
There's a twinkle in my Baby's eyes.

Sittin' around the campfire the river dances forever by
Meadow larks sing across the breeze
   Chance glimpse of a   firefly
Glow of the white hot coals
A lifelong memory unfolds
Moons peeking above the hill
Life and time by Mother Nature's will.

Sittin around the campfire fantastic tales are always told
From Purple Smoke to the Lady of Spain
   Stories range from young to old
Roar of the laughter
Makes happily forever and ever after
To the east a faint hint of light
The fire wanes. Peace. Goodnight.

It's Your Fortune
By Ben Racicot

One time fortune found me by a river
One time it found me at a lake
And two times fortune found me on my knees
Prayin for my baby's sake

One time fortune found me a wife
And then it blessed me with another
And four times fortune presented a daughter
Before then it blessed me with a mother

Fortune gave me my heart
And fortune gave me my eyes
Then fortune blessed me with a lesson
Not to worry 'bout what's gone by

Now I do believe I'm a fortunate son
I'm thankful for that everyday
And I'm quite certain that everyone
Can benefit from what I say

Fortune you see just happens to be
Appreciated seldom enough
It's fortune you see that everyone needs
To call on when times get tough

CHORUS
It's about all that you have, not what you don't
It's in the solace you did, Not the sorrow you won't
It's what you create, not what you hope
It's your fortune

It's in the smiles you find,
Not the tears you have cried
It's not the success, but what you learn while you try
It's the cheer in your laugh, Not the pity in your sigh
That's your fortune

CHORUS
It's about all that you have, not what you don't
It's in the solace you did, Not the sorrow you won't
It's what you create, not what you hope
It's your fortune

It's about finding your ease, never wanting to hide
It's contentment and peace and joy always implied
The day's only so long you gotta make it wide
It's your fortune

Family Song
By Ben Racicot

My momma's got macarena arm
When daddy sings he sets off alarms
And I'm quite certain that my grandpas on the "A"

Well my dog's blind and he's missin his tail
My screen door creaks, steps missin the rail
On the front porch where my brothers and me play

My yard is a treasure chest
Oddities daddy said passed the test
Of maybe being useful one rainy day

My sister swings is what I hear
But I can't find a playground near
Momma says her car blinkers are wired the wrong way

Well you might think my family's strange
But you'll never hear me complain
Friend I'll say your preachin' to the choir

Why just last week I awoke
with a cough and a gasp in a cloud of smoke
My brothers tried to light my bed on fire

Now I was told we're all one of a kind
Someone better than family you may never find
And I believe my momma ain't no liar

So your brother was born missin an ear
Your uncle's diet consists mostly of beer
And your quite certain your cousin looks at you
      the wrong way

Your TV only works at night
Your daddy thinks antennas are afraid of the light
And I never heard that so I really cannot say

Your cat is the neighborhood tramp
Your sister was sent home from summer camp
For disappearing too often in the stack of hay

Your gramma can't ever find her car
Late at night when she's leavin the bar
But you always walk with her to get it the next day

Well you might say your family's strange
But if I were you I would not complain
Friend some folks ain't got no family at all

Why just last week a boy I know
Was orphaned by events he couldn't control
Now he's got no one to pick him up should he fall

So I'll tell you Your family's one of a kind
Someone better than them you may never find
Friend be happy you got family on which to call

"Don't Fence Me In"

Also known as "Wildcat Kelly, was based on text by Robert (Bob) Fletcher who worked in Helena Montana as an engineer with the Department of Highways. In 1934 Cole Porter bought the poem from Bob Fletcher for $250.00 and created a musical score for the 20th Century Fox musical, "Adios Argentina". While the movie was never released, "Don't Fence Me In" became one of the most popular songs of the time.

~ ~ ~ ~ ~ ~ ~ ~

Wildcat Kelly, lookin' mighty pale
Was standin' by the Sherriff's side
And when that Sherriff said, "I'm sending you to jail"
Wildcat raised his head and cried

Oh, give me land, lots of land under starry skies above
Don't fence me in
Let me ride through the wide open country that I love
Don't fence me in

Let me be by myself in the evenin' breeze
And listen to the murmur of the cottonwood trees
Send me off forever but I ask you please
Don't fence me in

Just turn me loose, let me straddle my old saddle
Underneath the western skies
On my cayuse, let me wander over yonder
Till I see the mountains rise

I want to ride to the ridge where the west commences
And gaze at the moon till I lose my senses
I can't look at hobbles and I can't stand fences
Don't fence me in

248

Thanks

Mom and Dad for teaching me that life is an adventure. Thanks to each of my brothers and sisters, children and grandchildren, in-laws, nieces and nephews, cousins and friends who have taken this adventure with me.

Larry Racicot, the one I share my life, love and all my adventures with. For the Coffee, the Fire, the Food and the Laughter I will always be grateful.

Ben Racicot: for the Campfire Music
                    and editing assistance.

Kevin Michael Connolly: for editing assistance.

Marie Connolly: Who convinced me I could draw, I could paint and I could write!   I miss you every day!

The Dearborn and Lake Family and Friends:
        for the inspiration and encouragement.

The Highland Friends and Saturday Night Campfires

Dedication

To the people of Montana who exercise their right to vote for our right to access navigable rivers in Montana and Vote to maintain our right to use public land.

To the good stewards of Montana private lands who pay to maintain the roads and riverbanks
that get us where we want to go
and are gracious enough to share their view with us.

Finally, to our families and friends who make the Campfire Great in all ways!

CODE OF MONTANA

Pack it in, Pack it out!
Drown all Fires
Leave no Footprint
Be a good Neighbor
Protect our Public Land and Water

This book may be purchased at local Montana bookstores
and gift shops.Also on Amazon.com

For retail sales: please contact Peggy Racicot
mpraci@gmail.com2
453 West Shore Drive, Helena MT 59602

The Smith River, Montana

I was the third of eight children between the ages of one and ten. To preserve their sanity my parents opened the door and said "Go out and play".

I have hiked the mountains, I have floated the rivers and I have driven the backroads. I have planned the menus, done the shopping and cooked the food for 2 to 50 people.

Montana has always been and always will be my only home. I was born in Helena and lived in Great Falls, Missoula, and the Highlands of Butte. We have a family place on the Dearborn River and currently live on Canyon Ferry. My husbands parents also had a place on McGregor Lake near Libby. Each of these places own a piece of my heart.

To each of you, All The Best!

This is my first published book and certainly I have made mistakes. If you see something in need of correcting please let me know so I can correct it in the 2nd edition.
Love to hear your comments ~ mpraci@gmail.com

Made in the USA
Columbia, SC
30 May 2021